AN ADAPTED CLASSIC

MW01060014

A CHRISTMAS CAROL

CHARLES DICKENS

Globe
Fearon

Upper Saddle River,
New Jersey

Cover design: Marek Antoniak
Cover illustration: Cindy Spencer
Interior photos: Museum of Modern Art/Film Stills Archive

ISBN: 0-83590-028-2

Printed in the United States of America
8 9 10 04 03 02 01

ISBN: 0-835-90028-2

ABOUT THE AUTHOR

Charles Dickens was born in Portsmouth, England, in 1812. During his childhood, the family often was poor. When he was twelve, Dickens had to leave school and work in a shoe-polish factory. Although the experience lasted only a few months, Dickens never forgot how miserable he had been at this time. He later returned to school, but left for good when he was fifteen.

Dickens became a newspaper reporter, specializing in reports on the speeches and debates in Britain's Parliament. He also wrote feature articles, and his first book was a collection of these articles. His second book, *The Pickwick Papers*, was tremendously popular. At the age of 24, Dickens had become the most widely reader writer in the English language, a status that he held for the rest of his life.

Dickens wrote a large number of novels. Among the best known are *Oliver Twist, David Copperfield, Bleak House, Great Expectations,* and *A Tale of Two Cities*. He also wrote five short novels for the Christmas season, of which *A Christmas Carol* is the first and the most widely read.

Dickens also was an important magazine editor. In this role, he published the work of many younger writers for the first time. In his later years, Dickens gave many public readings of his books in Britain and America. He died in 1870.

PREFACE

When Dickens was writing *A Christmas Carol,* England was in the midst of industrialization, which led to great changes in the way people lived and worked. Small farms were turned into large estates and many peasants lost their land. Work that had once been done by hand was now performed by machines. More and more people were forced to leave rural field to work in urban factories. In cities such as London, life was harsh and unrewarding for the working class. Wages were low. Workdays were long. Few factory workers could read or write. As shortage of housing led to overcrowding and disease. The homeless of all ages were forced to live in workhouses, and crime flourished.

Dickens was very sympathetic to the poor, and depicted them honestly, although he frequently tended toward sentimentality. Scrooge, the selfish and miserly central character in *A Christmas Carol,* represented an extreme version of what was a common attitude among the better-off people of his time. His conversion from a mean-spirited businessman to an open-handed and cheerful giver is one of the most delightful and timeless stories in the English language.

Note: The book is divided into staves. This word is an old musical term. It is appropriate because a Christmas carol is, after all, a song.

ADAPTER'S NOTE

This adaptation maintains the style and flavor of Dickens's novel. No events important to the plot have been omitted. To make the story easier to understand, standard American spellings are used and certain long passages have been abridged. "Britishisms" have been clarified for American readers and some vocabulary has been simplified.

CONTENTS

STAVE ONE.

MARLEY'S GHOST.

MARLEY was dead, to begin with. There is no doubt whatever about that. The register of his burial was signed by the clergyman, the clerk, the undertaker, and the chief mourner. Scrooge signed it. And Scrooge's name was good for anything he chose to put his hand to. Old Marley was as dead as a doornail.

Scrooge knew he was dead? Of course he did. How could it be otherwise? Scrooge and he were partners for I don't know how many years. Scrooge was his sole executor, his sole administrator, his sole assign, his sole residuary legatee, his sole friend and sole mourner. And even Scrooge was not so dreadfully upset by the sad event. He was at work on the very day of the funeral, and solemnized it by striking a sharp bargain.

The mention of Marley's funeral brings me back to the point I started from. There is no doubt that Marley was dead. This must be distinctly understood, or nothing wonderful can come of the story I am going to relate.

Scrooge never painted out Old Marley's name. There it stood, years afterwards, above the warehouse door: Scrooge and Marley. The firm was known as Scrooge and Marley. Sometimes people

new to the business called Scrooge Scrooge, and
sometimes Marley, but he answered to both names.
It was all the same to him.

Oh! But Scrooge he was a tight-fisted man, a
squeezing, wrenching, grasping, scraping, clutching, covetous old sinner! Hard and sharp as flint,
from which no steel had ever struck out generous
fire. He was as secret, and self-contained, and solitary as an oyster. The cold within him froze his old
features, nipped his pointed nose, shrivelled his
cheek, stiffened his gait. It made his eyes red and
his thin lips blue. You could hear it in his grating
voice. A frost was on his head, and on his eyebrows,
and his wiry chin. He carried his own low tempera-
ture always about with him. He iced his office in
August and didn't thaw it one degree at Christmas.

External heat and cold had little influence on
Scrooge. No warmth could warm, nor wintry
weather chill him. No wind that blew was bitterer
than he. No falling snow was more intent upon its
purpose. No pelting rain less open to entreaty. Foul
weather didn't know where to have him. The heav-
iest rain, and snow, and hail, and sleet, could boast
of the advantage over him in only one respect.
They often "came down" handsomely, and Scrooge
never did.

Nobody ever stopped him in the street to say,
with pleasant looks, "My dear Scrooge, how are
you? When will you come to see me?" No beggars
implored him for a coin, no children asked him
what time it was, no man or woman ever once in
all his life asked directions of Scrooge. Even the
blindmen's dogs appeared to know him. When they
saw him coming they would tug their owners into

doorways. Then they would wag their tails as though they said, "No eye at all is better than an evil eye, dark master!"

But what did Scrooge care? It was the very thing he liked. To edge his way along the crowded paths of life, warning all human sympathy to keep its distance, was the way he wished to live.

Once upon a time—of all the good days in the year, on Christmas Eve—old Scrooge sat busy in his counting-house. It was cold, bleak, biting weather. He could hear the people in the court outside go wheezing up and down, stamping their feet upon the pavement-stones to warm them. The city clocks had only just rung three o'clock, but it was quite dark already. It had not been light all day. Candles were flaring in the windows of the neighboring offices. The fog came pouring in at every chink and keyhole. It was so densely foggy outside, that although the court was narrow, the houses opposite were mere phantoms.

The door of Scrooge's counting-house was open so that he could keep his eye upon his clerk, who was copying letters in a dismal little room beyond. Scrooge had a very small fire, but the clerk's fire was so very much smaller that it looked like one piece of coal. But he couldn't add to it, for Scrooge kept the coal-box in his own room. Any time the clerk came in with the shovel, Scrooge suggested that he was in danger of losing his job. So the clerk put on his white muffler and tried to warm himself at the candle. Not being a man of a strong imagination, he failed.

"A merry Christmas, uncle! God save you!" cried a cheerful voice. It was the voice of Scrooge's nephew, who came in so quickly that Scrooge had not seen his approach.

"Bah!" said Scrooge, "Humbug!"

Scrooge's nephew had so heated himself with rapid walking in the fog and frost that he was all in a glow. His face was ruddy and handsome. His eyes sparkled.

"Christmas a humbug, uncle!" said Scrooge's nephew. "You don't mean that, I am sure."

"I do," said Scrooge. "Merry Christmas! What right have you to be merry? What reason have you to be merry? You're poor enough."

"Come, then," returned the nephew cheerfully. "What right have you to be dismal? What reason have you to be gloomy? You're rich enough."

Scrooge having no better answer ready on the spur of the moment, said, "Bah!" again, and followed it up with "Humbug."

"Don't be cross, uncle," said the nephew.

"What else can I be," returned the uncle, "when I live in such a world of fools as this? Merry Christmas! Out upon merry Christmas! What's Christmas time to you but a time for paying bills without money; a time for finding yourself a year older, and not an hour richer; a time for balancing your books and discovering that you owe more than you have. If I could work my will," said Scrooge, indignantly, "every idiot who goes about with 'Merry Christmas' on his lips should be boiled with his own pudding, and buried with a stake of holly through his heart. He should!"

"Uncle!" pleaded the nephew.

"Nephew!" returned the uncle, sternly, "Keep Christmas in your own way, and let me keep it in mine."

"Keep it!" repeated Scrooge's nephew. "But you don't keep it."

"Let me leave it alone, then," said Scrooge. "Much good may it do you! Much good it has ever done you!"

"There are many things from which I might have derived good, by which I have not profited, I dare say," returned the nephew. "Christmas among the rest. But I am sure I have always thought of Christmas time, when it has come round as a good time. It's a kind, forgiving, charitable, pleasant time. It is the only time I know of, in the long calendar of the year, when men and women seem by to open their shut-up hearts freely, and to think of people below them as if they really were fellow-passengers to the grave, and not another race of creatures bound on other journeys. And therefore, uncle, though it has never put a scrap of gold or silver in my pocket, I believe that it has done me good, and will do me good. And I say, God bless it!"

The clerk in the tiny room involuntarily applauded. Becoming immediately aware that he should not have, he poked the fire. In so doing, he extinguished the last frail spark for ever.

"Let me hear another sound from you," said Scrooge to the clerk, "and you'll keep your Christmas by losing your job. You're quite a powerful speaker, sir," he added, turning to his nephew. "I wonder why you don't go into Parliament."

"Don't be angry, uncle. Come! Dine with us tomorrow."

Scrooge said that he would see him—yes, indeed he did. He said that he would see him in h—— first.

"But why?" cried Scrooge's nephew. "Why?"

"Why did you get married?" said Scrooge.

"Because I fell in love."

"Because you fell in love!" growled Scrooge, as if that were the only one thing in the world more ridiculous than a merry Christmas. "Good afternoon!"

"Nay, uncle, but you never came to see me before that happened. Why give it as a reason for not coming now?"

"Good afternoon," said Scrooge.

"I want nothing from you. I ask nothing of you. Why cannot we be friends?"

"Good afternoon," said Scrooge.

"I am sorry, with all my heart, to find you so resolute. We have never had any quarrel to which I have been a party. But I have made the effort because it is Christmas, and I'll keep my Christmas humour to the last. So a merry Christmas, uncle!"

"Good afternoon!" said Scrooge.

"And a happy New Year!"

"Good afternoon!" said Scrooge.

His nephew left the room without an angry word.

He stopped at the outer door to bestow the greetings of the season on the clerk. This poor fellow, cold as he was, was warmer than Scrooge, for he returned the greetings cordially.

"There's another fellow," muttered Scrooge, who had overheard him. "My clerk, with fifteen shillings a-week, and a wife and family, talking about a merry Christmas. I'll retire to a madhouse."

This lunatic, in letting Scrooge's nephew out, had let two other people in. They were portly gentlemen, pleasant to behold, and now stood, with their hats off, in Scrooge's office. They had books and papers in their hands, and bowed to him.

"Scrooge and Marley's, I believe," said one of the gentlemen, referring to his list. "Have I the pleasure of addressing Mr. Scrooge, or Mr. Marley?"

"Old Marley has been dead for seven years," Scrooge replied. "He died seven years ago, this very night."

"We have no doubt his generosity is well represented by his surviving partner," said the gentleman, presenting his credentials.

It certainly was, for Scrooge and Marley had been two kindred spirits. At the ominous word "generosity," Scrooge frowned, and shook his head, and handed the credentials back.

"At this festive season of the year, Mr. Scrooge," said the gentleman, taking up a pen, "it is poor and destitute who suffer greatly. Many thousands lack the necessities of life. Hundreds of thousands lack common comforts, sir."

"Are there no prisons?" asked Scrooge.

"Plenty of prisons," said the gentleman, laying down the pen again.

"And the union workhouses?" demanded Scrooge. "Are they still in operation?"

"They are. Still," returned the gentleman, "I wish I could say they were not."

"The Treadmill and the Poor Law are in full strength, then?" said Scrooge.

"Both very busy, sir."

"Oh! I was afraid, from what you said at first, that something had occurred to stop them in their useful course," said Scrooge. "I'm very glad to hear it."

"Knowing that these institutions do not give cheer of mind or body to those in need," returned the gentleman, "a few of us are trying to raise money to buy the poor some meat and drink, and means of warmth. We choose this time, because it is a time, of all others, when want is keenly felt, and Abundance rejoices. What shall I put you down for?"

"Nothing!" Scrooge replied.

"You wish to be anonymous?"

"I wish to be left alone," said Scrooge. "Since you ask me what I wish, gentlemen, that is my answer. I don't make merry myself at Christmas, and I can't afford to make idle people merry. I help to support the establishments I have mentioned. They cost enough, and those who are badly off must go there."

"Many can't go there—and many would rather die."

"If they would rather die," said Scrooge, "they had better do it, and decrease the surplus population. Besides—excuse me—I don't know that to be true."

"But you might know it," observed the gentleman.

"It's not my business," Scrooge returned. "It's enough for a man to understand his own business, and not to interfere with other people's. Mine occupies me constantly. Good afternoon, gentlemen!"

Seeing clearly that it would be useless to argue any more, the gentlemen left. Scrooge resumed his labours with an improved opinion of himself, and in a more cheerful temper than was usual with him.

Meanwhile the fog and darkness thickened so much that people ran about with flaring torches, offering their services to walk in front of horse-drawn carriages, and conduct them on their way. The ancient tower of a nearby church became invisible. Its gruff old bell struck the hours and quarters in the clouds. The vibrations afterwards sounded as if the bell's teeth were chattering in its frozen head up there. The cold became intense. In the main street, at the corner of the court, some labourers were repairing the gas-pipes. They had lighted a great fire in a metal barrel, around which a party of ragged men and boys were gathered. They were warming their hands and blinking their eyes before the blaze in rapture. The brightness of the shops, where holly sprigs and berries crackled in the lamp-heat of the windows, made pale faces ruddy as they passed. Poulterers' and grocers' trades became a splendid joke. They were such a glorious pageant that it was hard to believe that business had anything to do with it. The Lord Mayor, in the mighty Mansion House, gave orders to his fifty cooks and butlers to keep Christmas as a Lord Mayor's household should. Even the little tailor, whom the Lord Mayor had fined five shillings on the previous Monday for being drunk, stirred up to-morrow's pudding while his wife and the baby went out to buy the beef.

Foggier yet, and colder! Piercing, searching,

biting cold. One young boy gnawed by the hungry cold as bones are gnawed by dogs, stooped down at Scrooge's keyhole to regale him with a Christmas carol. But at the first sound of "God bless you merry gentleman! May nothing you dismay!" Scrooge seized a ruler with such speed that the singer fled in terror, leaving the keyhole to the fog and frost.

Finally the hour of shutting up the counting-house arrived. With an ill-will Scrooge got down from his stool. Seeing this, the clerk instantly snuffed his candle out, and put on his hat.

"You'll want all day tomorrow, I suppose?" said Scrooge.

"If quite convenient, sir."

"It's not convenient," said Scrooge, "and it's not fair. If I was to dock your pay half-a-crown for it, you'd think yourself ill used, I expect?"

The clerk smiled faintly.

"And yet," said Scrooge, "you don't think me ill-used when I pay a day's wages for no work."

The clerk observed that it was only once a year.

"A poor excuse for picking a man's pocket every twenty-fifth of December!" said Scrooge, buttoning his great-coat to the chin. "But I suppose you must have the whole day. Be here all the earlier next morning!"

The clerk promised that he would, and Scrooge walked out with a growl. The office was closed in a twinkling, and the clerk, with the long ends of his white muffler dangling below his waist (for he had no great-coat), ran home to Camden town as quickly as he could, to play at blindman's-buff.

Scrooge took his melancholy dinner in his usual melancholy tavern. Having read all the newspapers and whiled away the rest of the evening with his bank book, he went home to bed. He lived in chambers which had once belonged to his deceased partner. They were a gloomy suite of rooms, in a building in a dark courtyard, where it seemed out of place. It was old and dreary, for nobody lived in it but Scrooge. The other rooms were all rented out as offices. The courtyard was so dark that even Scrooge, who knew its every stone, had to grope with his hands to find his way to the door. The fog and frost hung about the black old gateway of the house. It seemed as if the weather sat in mournful meditation on the threshold.

Now, it is a fact that there was nothing at all particular about the knocker on the door, except that it was very large. It is also a fact that Scrooge had seen it every night and morning during the seven years that he had lived in that place. It is also true that Scrooge had as little imagination in him as any man in the City of London. Keep in mind that Scrooge had not thought of his dead partner Marley since mentioning him that afternoon. And then let any man explain to me, if he can, how it happened that Scrooge, having his key in the lock of the door, saw in the knocker, not a knocker, but Marley's face.

Marley's face. It was not in deep shadow as the other objects in the courtyard were. Instead, it had a dismal light about it. It was not angry or ferocious, but looked at Scrooge as Marley used to look. It had with ghostly spectacles turned up upon its ghostly forehead. The hair was curiously moved, as if by breath or hot air. Yet, though the eyes were wide open, they were perfectly motionless. That, and its livid colour, made it horrible. But its horror seemed to be beyond its control, rather than a part of its own expression.

As Scrooge stared at this phenomenon, it was a knocker again.

To say that he was not startled, or that his blood had not run cold, would be untrue. But he turned the key firmly, walked in, and lighted his candle.

He did pause, with a moment's hesitation, before he shut the door. And he did look cautiously behind it first, as if he half-expected to see the back of Marley's head sticking out into the hall. But there was nothing on the back of the door, except the screws and nuts that held the knocker on. So he said "Pooh, pooh!" and closed it with a bang.

The sound resounded through the house like thunder. Every room above, and every cask in the wine-merchant's cellars below, appeared to have a separate set of echoes of its own. Scrooge was not a man to be frightened by echoes. He fastened the door, and walked across the hall, and up the stairs. He walked slowly too, trimming his candle as he went.

The stairs were extremely wide, which is perhaps the reason why Scrooge thought he saw a hearse going on before him in the gloom. Half a dozen gas-lamps out of the street wouldn't have lighted the entry too well, so you may suppose that it was pretty dark.

Up Scrooge went, not caring a button for that.

Darkness is cheap, and Scrooge liked it. But before he shut his heavy door, he walked through his rooms to see that all was right. He had just enough recollection of the face to desire to do that.

Sitting-room, bed-room, lumber-room. All as they should be. Nobody under the table, nobody under the sofa. A small fire in the grate; spoon and basin ready; and the little saucepan of gruel (Scrooge had a cold in his head) on the back of the stove. Nobody under the bed; nobody in the closet. Nobody in his dressing-gown, which was hanging up in a suspicious attitude against the wall. Lumber-room as usual. Old fire-guard, old shoes, two fish-baskets, washing-stand on three legs, and a poker.

Quite satisfied, he closed his door and locked himself in. In fact, he double-locked himself in, which was not his habit. Thus secured against surprise, he took off his cravat. Then he put on his dressing-gown and slippers, and his night-cap. He sat down before the fire to take his gruel.

It was a very low fire indeed, not enough for such a bitter night. He was obliged to sit close to it, and brood over it, before he could feel the least sensation of warmth from such a handful of fuel. The fireplace was an old one, built by some Dutch merchant long ago, and paved all round with quaint Dutch tiles, designed to illustrate the scriptures. There were Cains and Abels; Pharaoh's daughters, Queens of Sheba, Angelic messengers descending through the air on clouds like feather-beds, Abrahams, Belshazzars, Apostles putting off to sea in boats, hundreds of figures to attract his thoughts. Yet, that face of Marley, seven years dead, swallowed up the whole. If each smooth tile had been a blank at first, with power to shape some picture on its surface from Scrooge's thoughts, there would have been a copy of old Marley's head on every one.

"Humbug!" said Scrooge. He walked across the room.

After several turns, he sat down again. As he threw his head back in the chair, his glance happened to rest upon a bell that hung in the room but was never used. The bell had once communicated for some purpose now forgotten with a chamber in the highest story of the building. It was with great astonishment, and with a strange feeling of dread, that he saw this bell begin to swing. It swung so softly at first that it scarcely made a sound. But soon it rang out loudly, and so did every bell in the house.

This might have lasted half a minute, or a minute, but it seemed an hour. The bells ceased as they had begun, together. They were succeeded by a clanking noise, deep down below, as if some person were dragging a heavy chain over the casks in the wine-merchant's cellar. Scrooge then remembered to have heard that ghosts in haunted houses were described as dragging chains.

The cellar door flew open with a booming sound, and then he heard the noise much louder, on the floors below, then coming up the stairs, then coming straight towards his door.

"It's humbug still!" said Scrooge. "I won't believe it."

His colour changed though, when, without a pause, it came on through the heavy door, and

passed into the room before his eyes. Upon its coming in, the dying flame leaped up, as though it cried "I know him! Marley's Ghost!" and fell again.

The same face, the very same. Marley in his usual waistcoat, tights, boots, and coat, and the hair upon his head. The chain he drew was clasped about his middle. It was long, and wound about him like a tail. It was made (for Scrooge observed it closely) of cashboxes, keys, padlocks, ledgers, deeds, and heavy purses wrought in steel. His body was transparent, so that Scrooge, observing him, and looking through his waistcoat, could see the two buttons on the back of his coat.

Scrooge had often heard it said that Marley had no guts, but he had never believed it until now.

No, nor did he believe it even now. Though he looked the phantom through and through, and saw it standing before him, he did not believe what he saw. Though he felt the chilling influence of its death-cold eyes and noticed the very texture of the folded kerchief bound about its head and chin, he still would not believe. He fought against his senses.

"How now!" said Scrooge, caustic and cold as ever. "What do you want with me?"

"Much!" Marley's voice, no doubt about it.

"Who are you?"

"Ask me who I was."

"Who were you, then?" said Scrooge, raising his voice. "You're particular—for a ghost."

"In life I was your partner, Jacob Marley."

"Can you—can you sit down?" asked Scrooge, looking doubtfully at him.

"I can."

"Do it then."

Scrooge asked the question, because he didn't know whether a ghost so transparent might be able to sit in a chair. He did not wish to embarrass the Ghost. But the Ghost sat down on the opposite side of the fireplace, as if he were quite used to it.

"You don't believe in me," observed the Ghost.

"I don't," said Scrooge.

"What evidence would you have of my reality, beyond that of your senses?"

"I don't know," said Scrooge.

"Why do you doubt your senses?"

"Because," said Scrooge, "the least little thing affects them. A slight disorder of the stomach makes them cheats. You may be an undigested bit of beef, a blot of mustard, a crumb of cheese, a fragment of an underdone potato. There's more of gravy than of grave about you, whatever you are!"

Scrooge was not much in the habit of cracking jokes, nor did he feel, in his heart, very witty. The truth is that he tried to be smart as a means of distracting his own attention and keeping down his terror. For the spectre's voice disturbed the very marrow in his bones.

To sit silently for a moment, staring at those fixed, glazed eyes, Scrooge felt, would be his undoing. There was something very awful, too, in the spectre's being provided with an infernal atmosphere of its own. Scrooge could not feel it himself, but this was clearly the case. For though the Ghost sat perfectly motionless, its hair, and coat, and the tassels of its boots, were still moving, as by the hot vapour from an oven.

"You see this toothpick?" said Scrooge,

returning quickly to the charge, and wishing, though it were only for a second, to divert the vision's stony gaze from himself.

"I do," replied the Ghost.

"You are not looking at it," said Scrooge.

"But I see it," said the Ghost, "notwithstanding."

"Well!" returned Scrooge. "I have but to swallow this, and be for the rest of my days persecuted by a legion of goblins, all of my own creation. Humbug, I tell you—humbug!"

At this, the Spirit raised a frightful cry, and shook its chain with such a dismal and appalling noise, that Scrooge held on tight to his chair, to save himself from fainting. But how much greater was his horror, when the phantom took off the bandage round its head and its lower jaw dropped down upon its breast!

Scrooge fell upon his knees, and clasped his hands before his face.

"Mercy!" he said. "Dreadful apparition, why do you trouble me?"

"Man of the worldly mind!" replied the Ghost, "Do you believe in me or not?"

"I do," said Scrooge. "I must. But why do spirits walk the earth, and why do they come to me?"

"It is required of every man," the Ghost returned, "that the spirit within him should walk abroad among his fellowmen, and travel far and wide. If that spirit goes not forth in life, it is condemned to do so after death. It is doomed to wander through the world—oh, woe is me!—and witness what it cannot share, but might have shared on earth, and turned to happiness!"

Again the spectre raised a cry, and shook its chain, and wrung its shadowy hands.

"You are chained," said Scrooge, trembling. "Tell me why?"

"I wear the chain I forged in life," replied the Ghost. "I made it link by link, and yard by yard. I girded it on of my own free will, and of my own free will I wore it. Is its pattern strange to you?"

Scrooge trembled more and more.

"Or would you know," pursued the Ghost, "the weight and length of the strong coil you bear yourself? It was full as heavy and as long as this, seven Christmas Eves ago. You have laboured on it, since. It is a ponderous chain!"

Scrooge glanced about him on the floor, in the expectation of finding himself surrounded by some fifty or sixty fathoms of iron cable. But he could see nothing.

"Jacob," he said, imploringly. "Old Jacob Marley, tell me more. Speak comfort to me, Jacob."

"I have none to give," the Ghost replied. "It comes from other regions, Ebenezer Scrooge, and is conveyed by other ministers, to other kinds of men. Nor can I tell you what I would. A very little more, is all permitted to me. I cannot rest, I cannot stay, I cannot linger anywhere. My spirit never walked beyond our counting-house. Mark me! In life my spirit never roved beyond the narrow limits of our money-changing hole; and weary journeys lie before me!"

It was a habit with Scrooge, whenever he became thoughtful, to put his hands in his breeches pockets. Pondering on what the Ghost had said, he did so now, but without lifting up his eyes, or getting off his knees.

"You must have been very slow about it, Jacob," Scrooge observed, in a business-like manner, though with humility and deference.

"Slow!" the Ghost repeated.

"Seven years dead," mused Scrooge. "And travelling all the time?"

"The whole time," said the Ghost. "No rest, no peace. Incessant torture of remorse."

"You travel fast?" said Scrooge.

"On the wings of the wind," replied the Ghost.

"You might have got over a great quantity of ground in seven years," said Scrooge.

The Ghost, on hearing this, set up another cry, and clanked its chain hideously in the dead silence of the night.

"Oh! captive, bound, and double-ironed," cried the phantom, "not to know that any good spirit working kindly in its little sphere, whatever it may be, will find its mortal life too short for its vast means of usefulness. Not to know that no space of regret can make amends for one life's opportunities misused! Yet such was I! Oh! such was I!"

"But you were always a good man of business, Jacob," faltered Scrooge, who now began to apply this to himself.

"Business!" cried the Ghost, wringing its hands again. "Mankind was my business. The common welfare was my business. Charity, mercy, forbearance, and benevolence, were all my business. The dealings of my trade were but a drop of water in the comprehensive ocean of my business!"

It held up its chain at arm's length, as if that

were the cause of all its unavailing grief, and flung it heavily upon the ground again.

"At this time of the year," the spectre said, "I suffer most. Why did I walk through crowds of fellow beings with my eyes turned down, and never raise them to that blessed star which led the Wise Men to a poor abode? Were there no poor homes to which its light would have taken me?"

Scrooge was very much dismayed to hear the spectre going on like this, and began to quake.

"Hear me!" cried the Ghost. "My time is nearly gone."

"I will," said Scrooge. "But don't be hard upon me! Don't be flowery, Jacob! Pray!"

"How it is that I appear before you in a shape that you can see, I may not tell. I have sat invisible beside you many and many a day."

It was not an agreeable idea. Scrooge shivered, and wiped the perspiration from his brow.

"That is no light part of my penance," pursued the Ghost. "I am here tonight to warn you, that you have yet a chance and hope of escaping my fate. A chance and hope that I have obtained for you, Ebenezer."

"You were always a good friend to me," said Scrooge. "Thank'ee!"

"You will be haunted," resumed the Ghost, "by Three Spirits."

Scrooge's face fell almost as low as the Ghost's had done.

"Is that the chance and hope you mentioned, Jacob?" he demanded, in a faltering voice.

"It is."

"I—I think I'd rather not," said Scrooge.

"Without their visits," said the Ghost, "you cannot hope to shun the path I tread. Expect the first tomorrow, when the bell tolls one."

"Couldn't I take 'em all at once, and have it over, Jacob?" hinted Scrooge.

"Expect the second on the next night at the same hour. The third upon the next night when the last stroke of twelve has ceased to vibrate. Look to see me no more. Remember what has passed between us!"

When it had said these words, the spectre took its wrapper from the table, and bound it round its head, as before. Scrooge knew this, by the snapping sound its teeth made, when the jaws were brought together by the bandage. He ventured to raise his eyes again, and found his supernatural visitor standing before him, with its chain wound over and about its arm.

The apparition walked backward from him. At every step it took, the window raised itself a little, so that when the spectre reached it, it was wide open. It beckoned Scrooge to approach, which he did. When they were within two paces of each other, Marley's Ghost held up its hand, warning him to come no nearer. Scrooge stopped.

Not so much in obedience, as in surprise and fear. For on the raising of the hand, he became aware of confused noises in the air. There were incoherent sounds of lamentation and regret, wailings inexpressibly sorrowful and self-accusatory. The spectre, after listening for a moment, joined in the mournful dirge and floated out upon the bleak, dark night.

Scrooge followed it to the window. He was

desperate in his curiosity. He looked out.

The air was filled with phantoms, wandering hither and thither in restless haste, and moaning as they went. Every one of them wore chains like Marley's Ghost. Some few (they might be guilty governments) were linked together. None were free. Many had begen personally known to Scrooge in their lives. He had been quite familiar with one old ghost, in a white waistcoat, with a monstrous iron safe attached to its ankle, who cried piteously at being unable to assist a wretched woman with an infant, whom it saw below, upon a doorstep. The misery with them all was, clearly, that they sought to interfere, for good, in human matters, and had lost the power for ever.

Whether these creatures faded into mist, or mist enshrouded them, he could not tell. But they and their spirit voices faded together, and the night became as it had been when he walked home.

Scrooge closed the window, and examined the door by which the Ghost had entered. It was double-locked, as he had locked it with his own hands, and the bolts were undisturbed. He tried to say "Humbug!" but stopped at the first syllable. And being, from the emotion he had undergone, or the fatigues of the day, or his glimpse of the invisible world, or the dull conversation of the Ghost, or the lateness of the hour, badly in need of sleep, he went straight to bed, without undressing, and fell asleep instantly.

STAVE TWO.

THE FIRST OF THE THREE SPIRITS.

When Scrooge awoke, it was so dark that, looking out of bed, he could scarcely distinguish the transparent window from the solid walls of his chamber. He was trying to pierce the darkness with his sharp eyes when the chimes of a neighbouring church struck the four quarters. So he listened for the hour.

To his great astonishment the heavy bell went on from six to seven, and from seven to eight, and regularly up to twelve. Then it stopped. Twelve! It was past two when he went to bed. The clock was wrong. An icicle must have got into the works. Twelve!

He touched the spring of his watch, to correct this most preposterous clock. Its rapid little pulse beat twelve and stopped.

"Why, it isn't possible," said Scrooge, "that I can have slept through a whole day and far into another night. It isn't possible that anything has happened to the sun, and this is twelve at noon!"

The idea being an alarming one, he scrambled out of bed, and groped his way to the window. He had to rub the frost off with the sleeve of his dressing-gown before he could see anything. He could see very little even then. All he could make out was that it was still very foggy and extremely cold, and that there was no noise of people about as there would have been if it were daytime. This was a great relief, because "in three days pay to Mr. Ebenezer Scrooge or his order," and so forth, would have become worthless if there were no days to count by.

Scrooge went to bed again, and thought, and thought, and thought it over and over and over, and could make nothing of it. The more he thought, the more confused he was. The more he tried not to think, the more he thought. Marley's Ghost bothered him exceedingly. Every time he decided that it was all a dream, his mind flew back again to its first position, and presented the same problem to be worked all through, "Was it a dream or not?"

Scrooge lay in this state until the chimes had gone three quarters of an hour more. Then he suddenly remembered that the Ghost had warned him of a visitation when the bell tolled one. He resolved to lie awake until the hour was past. Considering that he could no more go to sleep than go to Heaven, this was perhaps the wisest decision he could have made.

The quarter hour was so long that he was more than once convinced he must have sunk into a doze unconsciously, and missed the chimes of the clock. At length it broke upon his listening ear.

"Ding, dong!"

"A quarter past," said Scrooge, counting.

"Ding, dong!"

"Half past!" said Scrooge.

"Ding, dong!"

"A quarter to it," said Scrooge.

"Ding, dong!"

"The hour itself," said Scrooge, triumphantly, "and nothing else!"

He spoke before the hour bell sounded, which it now did with a deep, dull, hollow, melancholy ONE. Light flashed up in the room instantly, and the curtains of his bed were drawn.

The curtains of his bed were drawn aside, I tell you, by a hand. Not the curtains at his feet, nor the curtains at his back, but those to which his face was turned. The curtains of his bed were drawn aside. Scrooge, starting to sit up, found himself face to face with the unearthly visitor who drew them. He was as close to it as I am now to you, and I am standing in spirit at your elbow.

It was a strange figure. It was like a child. Yet, it was not so much like a child as like an old man, seen through some supernatural medium. This medium gave him the appearance of being far away and therefore seeming as small as a child. Its hair, which hung about its neck and down its back, was white as if with age. Yet, the face had not a wrinkle in it, and the tenderest bloom was on the skin. The arms were very long and muscular. The hands were the same, as if its hold were of uncommon strength. Its legs and feet, most delicately formed, were bare. It wore a tunic of the purest white. Round its waist was bound a lustrous belt, the sheen of which was beautiful. It held a branch of fresh green holly in its hand. Its tunic was trimmed with summer flowers. But the strangest thing about it was, that from the crown of its head there sprung a bright clear jet of light, by which all this was visible. This was probably why it used, in its duller moments, a great extinguisher for a cap, which it now held under its arm.

Even this, though, when Scrooge looked at it with increasing steadiness, was not its strangest quality. For as its belt sparkled and glittered now in one part and now in another, and what was light one instant, at another time was dark, so the figure itself changed constantly. Now it was a thing with one arm, now with one leg, now with twenty legs. Now it was a pair of legs without a head, now a head without a body. As its parts dissolved, no outline could be seen in the dense gloom into which they melted away. Then suddenly it would be itself again, distinct and clear as ever.

"Are you the Spirit, sir, whose coming was foretold to me?" asked Scrooge.

"I am!"

The voice was soft and gentle. Singularly low, as if instead of being so close beside him, it were at a distance.

"Who, and what are you?" Scrooge demanded.

"I am the Ghost of Christmas Past."

"Long past?" inquired Scrooge, observant of its dwarfish stature.

"No. Your past."

Scrooge could not have told anybody why, but he had a special desire to see the spirit in his cap. He begged him to put it on.

"What!" exclaimed the Ghost, "Would you so soon put out, with worldly hands, the light I give? Is it not enough that you are one of those whose passions made this cap, and force me through whole trains of years to wear it low upon my brow!"

Scrooge reverently disclaimed all intention to offend, or any knowledge of having willfully "bonneted" the spirit at any period of his life. He then asked what business brought him there.

"Your welfare!" said the Ghost.

Scrooge expressed himself much obliged, but could not help thinking that a night of unbroken rest would have been better for him. The Spirit must have heard him thinking, for it said immediately:

"Your salvation, then. Take heed!"

It put out its strong hand as it spoke, and clasped him gently by the arm.

"Rise! and walk with me!"

It would have been in vain for Scrooge to plead that the weather and the hour were not suitable for a walk. It would have been pointless for him to say that bed was warm, and the thermometer a long way below freezing, that he was wearing only slippers, dressing-gown, and nightcap, and that he had a head-cold. The grasp, though gentle as a woman's hand, was not to be resisted. He rose, but finding that the spirit made towards the window, clasped its robe in supplication.

"I am a mortal," Scrooge cried, "and liable to fall."

"Bear but a touch of my hand there," said the Spirit, laying it upon his heart, "and you shall be upheld in more than this!"

As the words were spoken, they passed through the wall, and stood upon an open country road, with fields on either hand. The city had entirely vanished. Not a vestige of it was to be

seen. The darkness and the mist had vanished with it, for it was a clear, cold, winter day, with snow upon the ground.

"Good Heaven!" said Scrooge, clasping his hands together, as he looked about him. "I was bred in this place. I was a boy here!"

The Spirit gazed upon him mildly. Its gentle touch, though it had been light and instantaneous, appeared still present to the old man's sense of feeling. He was conscious of a thousand odors floating in the air, each one connected with a thousand thoughts, and hopes, and joys, and cares long, long, forgotten!

"Your lip is trembling," said the Ghost. "And what is that upon your cheek?"

Scrooge muttered, with an unusual catching in his voice, that it was a pimple. He begged the Ghost to lead him where he would.

"You remember the way?" inquired the spirit.

"Remember it!" cried Scrooge with fervor. "I could walk it blindfold."

"Strange to have forgotten it for so many years!" observed the Ghost. "Let us go on."

They walked along the road. Scrooge recognized every gate, and post, and tree. A a little market-town appeared in the distance, with its bridge, its church, and winding river. Some shaggy ponies now were seen trotting towards them with boys upon their backs, who called to other boys in country gigs and carts, driven by farmers. All these boys were in great spirits, and shouted to each other, until the broad fields were so full of merry music, that the crisp air laughed to hear it.

"These are but shadows of the things that have

been," said the Ghost. "They have no consciousness of us."

The happy travellers came nearer. As they came, Scrooge knew and named them every one. Why was he rejoiced beyond all bounds to see them? Why did his cold eye glisten, and his heart leap up as they went past? Why was he filled with gladness when he heard them give each other Merry Christmas, as they parted at cross-roads and bye-ways, for their several homes? What was merry Christmas to Scrooge? Out upon merry Christmas! What good had it ever done to him?

"The school is not quite deserted," said the Ghost. "A solitary child, neglected by his friends, is left there still."

Scrooge said he knew it. And he sobbed.

They left the high-road, by a well remembered lane, and soon approached a mansion of dull red brick, with a little cupola on the roof, and a bell hanging in it. It was a large house, but one of broken fortunes. For the spacious offices were little used, their walls were damp and mossy, their windows broken, and their gates decayed. Hens clucked and strutted in the stables; and the coach-houses and sheds were over-run with grass. Nor was it better-kept inside. Entering the dreary hall and glancing through the open doors of many rooms, they found them poorly furnished, cold, and vast. There was an earthly flavour in the air, a chilly bareness in the place, which associated itself somehow with too much getting up by candlelight, and not too much to eat.

They went, the Ghost and Scrooge, across the hall, to a door at the back of the house. It opened before them. There was a long, bare, sad-looking room, made barer still by lines and desks. At one of these a lonely boy was reading near a feeble fire. Scrooge sat down upon a bench, and wept to see his poor forgotten self as he had used to be.

Not a latent echo in the house, not a squeak and scuffle from the mice behind the panelling, not a drip from the half-thawed water-spout in the dull yard behind, not a sigh among the leafless boughs of one old tree not the idle swinging of an empty store-house door, no, not a clicking in the fire, but fell upon the heart of Scrooge with softening influence, and gave a freer passage to his tears.

The spirit touched him on the arm, and pointed to his younger self, intent upon his reading. Suddenly a man in foreign garments stood outside the window, with an axe stuck in his belt, and leading a donkey laden with wood. He seemed wonderfully real.

"Why, it's Ali Baba!" Scrooge exclaimed in ecstasy "It's dear old honest Ali Baba! Yes, yes, I know! One Christmas time, when yonder solitary child was left here all alone, he did come, for the first time, just like that. Poor boy! And Valentine," said Scrooge, "and his wild brother, Orson. There they go! And what's his name, who was put down in his drawers, asleep, at the Gate of Damascus. Don't you see him? And the Sultan's Groom turned upside down by the Genii. There he is upon his head! Served him right. I'm glad of it. What business had he to be married to the Princess!"

To hear Scrooge expending all the earnestness of his nature on such imaginary subjects would have been a surprise to his business friends in the city, indeed.

"There's the parrot!" cried Scrooge. "Green body and yellow tail, with a thing like a lettuce growing out of the top of his head? There he is! Poor Robin Crusoe, he called him, when he came home again after sailing round the island. 'Poor Robin Crusoe, where have you been, Robin Crusoe?' The man thought he was dreaming, but he wasn't. It was the Parrot, you know. There goes Friday, running for his life to the little creek! Halloa! Hoop! Halloo!"

Then, with a change of mood very foreign to his usual character, he said, in pity for his former self, "Poor boy!" and cried again.

"I wish," Scrooge muttered, putting his hand in his pocket, and looking about him, after drying his eyes with his cuff. "but it's too late now."

"What is the matter?" asked the spirit.

"Nothing," said Scrooge. "Nothing. There was a boy singing a Christmas carol at my door last night. I should like to have given him something, that's all."

The Ghost smiled thoughtfully, and waved its hand, saying as it did so, "Let us see another Christmas!"

Scrooge's former self grew larger at the words, and the room became a little darker and more dirty. The panels shrunk, the windows cracked. Fragments of plaster fell out of the ceiling, and the laths showed instead. How all this was brought about, Scrooge knew no more than you do. He only knew that it was quite correct, that everything had happened so. He knew that there he was, alone again, when all the other boys had gone home for the jolly holidays.

He was not reading now, but walking up and down despairingly. Scrooge looked at the Ghost, and with a mournful shaking of his head, glanced anxiously towards the door.

It opened, and a little girl, much younger than the boy, came darting in. Putting her arms about his neck, and often kissing him, she addressed him as her "Dear, dear brother."

"I have come to bring you home, dear brother!" said the child, clapping her tiny hands, and bending down to laugh. "to bring you home, home, home!"

"Home, little Fan?" returned the boy.

"Yes!" said the child, brimful of glee. "Home, for good and all. Home, for ever and ever. Father is so much kinder than he used to be, that home's like Heaven! He spoke so gently to me one night when I was going to bed, that I was not afraid to ask him once more if you might come home. And he said yes, you should, and sent me in a coach to bring you. And you're to be a man!" said the child, opening her eyes, "and are never to come back here. But first, we're to be together all the Christmas long, and have the merriest time in all the world."

"You are quite a woman, little Fan!" exclaimed the boy.

She clapped her hands and laughed. She tried to touch his face, but being too little, laughed again, and stood on tiptoe to embrace him. Then she began to drag him, in her childish eagerness, towards the door. He eagerly accompanied her.

A terrible voice in the hall cried, "Bring down

Master Scrooge's box, there!" In the hall appeared the school-master himself, who glared on Master Scrooge with a ferocious condescension, and threw him into a dreadful state of mind by shaking hands with him. He then conveyed him and his sister into the coldest and dreariest parlour that ever was seen, where the maps upon the wall, and the celestial and terrestrial globes in the windows, were waxy with cold. Here he produced a pot of curiously weak tea and a block of curiously heavy cake. He served some of those dainties to the young people. At the same time, he sent out a thin servant to offer a glass of "something" to the postboy. The postboy answered that he thanked the gentleman, but if it was the same thing that he had tasted before, he had rather not. Master Scrooge's trunk being by this time tied on to the top of the chaise, the children bade the schoolmaster good-bye very willingly. Getting into it, they drove happily down the lane. The quick wheels dashed the frost and snow from the dark leaves of the evergreens like spray.

"Always a delicate creature, whom a breath might have withered," said the Ghost. "But she had a large heart!"

"So she had," cried Scrooge. "You're right. I'll not deny it, spirit. God forbid!"

"She died a woman," said the Ghost, "and had, as I think, children."

"One child," Scrooge returned.

"True," said the Ghost. "Your nephew!"

Scrooge seemed uneasy in his mind, and answered briefly, "Yes."

Although they had just left the school behind

them, they were now in the busy streets of a city, where shadowy passengers passed and repassed. Shadowy carts and coaches battled for the right of way. And all the strife and tumult of a real city was there. It was made plain enough, by the windows of the shops, that here too it was Christmas time again. It was evening though, and the streets were lighted up.

The Ghost stopped at a certain warehouse door, and asked Scrooge if he knew it.

"Know it!" said Scrooge. "Was I apprenticed here?"

They went in. At sight of an old gentleman in a Welch wig, sitting behind such a high desk, Scrooge cried in great excitement:

"Why, it's old Fezziwig! Bless his heart. It's Fezziwig alive again!"

Old Fezziwig laid down his pen, and looked up at the clock, which pointed to the hour of seven. He rubbed his hands and adjusted his large waistcoat. He laughed heartily and called out in a comfortable, oily, rich, fat, jovial voice:

"Yo ho, there! Ebenezer! Dick!"

Scrooge's former self, now grown a young man, came briskly in, accompanied by his fellow apprentice.

"Dick Wilkins, to be sure!" said Scrooge to the Ghost. "Bless me, yes. There he is. He was very much attached to me, was Dick. Poor Dick! Dear, dear!"

"Yo ho, my boys!" said Fezziwig. "No more work tonight. Christmas Eve, Dick. Christmas, Ebenezer! Let's have the shutters up," cried old Fezziwig, with a sharp clap of his hands "before a man can say Jack Robinson!"

You wouldn't believe how those two fellows went at it! They charged into the street with the shutters—one, two, three—had 'em up in their places—four, five, six—barred 'em and pinned 'em—seven, eight, nine—and came back before you could have got to twelve, panting like race-horses.

"Hilli-ho!" cried old Fezziwig, skipping down from the high desk with wonderful agility. "Clear away, my lads, and let's have lots of room here! Hilli-ho, Dick! Chirrup, Ebenezer!"

Clear away! There was nothing they wouldn't have cleared away, or couldn't have cleared away, with old Fezziwig looking on. It was done in a minute. Every movable was packed off, as if it were dismissed from public life for evermore. The floor was swept and mopped, the lamps were trimmed, fuel was heaped upon the fire. The warehouse was as snug, and warm, and dry, and bright a ballroom as you would desire to see upon a winter's night.

In came a fiddler with a musicbook, and went up to the lofty desk, and made an orchestra of it. In came Mrs. Fezziwig, one vast substantial smile. In came the three Miss Fezziwigs, beaming and lovable. In came the six young men whose hearts they broke. In came all the young men and women employed in the business. In came the housemaid, with her cousin, the baker. In came the cook, with her brother's best friend, the milkman. In came the boy from over the way, who was suspected of not being fed enough by his master. He was trying to hide himself behind the girl from next door. In they all came, one after another. Some came in shyly, some boldly, some gracefully, some awkwardly, some pushing, some pulling. In they all came, anyhow and everyhow. Away they all danced, twenty couples at once, hands half round and back again the other way. They danced down the middle and up again round and round. The old top couple always turned up in the wrong place. The new top couple started off again, as soon as they got there. All top couples arrived at last, and not a bottom one to help them. When this result was brought about, old Fezziwig, clapping his hands to stop the dance, cried out, "Well done!" and the fiddler plunged his hot face into a pot of porter especially provided for that purpose. Scorning rest, he instantly began again, though there were no dancers yet. It was as if the other fiddler had been carried home, exhausted, and he were a brand new man determined to outdo him or die trying.

There were more dancers, and more dances, and there was cake, and there was punch, and there was a great piece of cold roast beef, and there was a great piece of cold boiled beef, and there were mincepies, and plenty of beer. But the great effect of the evening came after the roast and boiled, when the fiddler (an artful dog, mind! the sort of man who knew his business better than you or I could have told it him!) struck up "Sir Roger de Coverley." Then old Fezziwig stood out to dance with Mrs. Fezziwig. Top couple too, with a good stiff piece of work cut out for them. Three or four and twenty pair of partners, people who were not to be trifled with. People who would dance, and had no notion of walking.

But if they had been twice as many—ah, four times—old Fezziwig would have been a match for them, and so would Mrs. Fezziwig. As to her, she was worthy to be his partner in every sense of the term. If that's not high praise, tell me higher, and I'll use it. A positive light appeared to issue from Fezziwig's legs. They shone in every part of the dance like beacons. You couldn't have predicted, at any given time, what would become of 'em next. And when old Fezziwig and Mrs. Fezziwig had gone all through the dance, Fezziwig appeared to wink with his legs, and came upon his feet again without a stagger.

When the clock struck eleven, this domestic ball broke up. Mr. and Mrs. Fezziwig took their stations, one on either side of the door, and shaking hands with every person individually as he or she went out, wished him or her a Merry Christmas. When everybody had retired but the two apprentices, they did the same to them. Thus the cheerful voices died away, and the lads were left to their beds, which were under a counter in the back-shop.

During the whole of this time, Scrooge had acted like a man out of his wits. His heart and soul were in the scene, and with his former self. He corroborated everything, remembered everything, enjoyed everything, and underwent the strangest agitation. It was not until now, when the bright faces of his former self and Dick were turned from them, that he remembered the Ghost, and became conscious that it was looking full upon him, while the light upon its head burnt very clear.

"A small matter," said the Ghost, "to make these silly folks so full of gratitude."

"Small!" echoed Scrooge.

The Spirit signed to him to listen to the two apprentices, who were pouring out their hearts in praise of Fezziwig. When Scrooge had done so, the Spirit said:

"Why! Is it not? He has spent but a few pounds of your mortal money—three or four, perhaps. Is that so much that he deserves this praise?"

"It isn't that," said Scrooge, heated by the remark, and speaking unconsciously like his former, not his latter, self. "It isn't that, Spirit. He has the power to render us happy or unhappy, to make our service light or burdensome, a pleasure or a toil. Say that his power lies in words and looks, in things so slight and insignificant that it is impossible to add and count 'em up. What then? The happiness he gives is quite as great as if it cost a fortune."

He felt the spirit's glance, and stopped.

"What is the matter?" asked the Ghost.

"Nothing particular," said Scrooge.

"Something, I think?" the Ghost insisted.

"No," said Scrooge, "No. I should like to be able to say a word or two to my clerk just now! That's all."

His former self turned down the lamps as he gave utterance to the wish. Scrooge and the ghost once again stood side by side in the open air.

"My time grows short," observed the spirit. "Quick!"

This was not addressed to Scrooge, or to any

one whom he could see, but it produced an immediate effect. For again Scrooge saw himself. He was older now; a man in the prime of life. His face had not the harsh and rigid lines of later years, but it had begun to wear the signs of care and avarice. There was an eager, greedy, restless motion in the eye, which showed the passion that had taken root, and where the shadow of the growing tree would fall.

He was not alone, but sat by the side of a fair young girl in a mourning-dress. In her eyes there were tears, which sparkled in the light that shone out of the Ghost of Christmas past.

"It matters little," she said, softly. "to you, very little. Another idol has displaced me. If it can cheer and comfort you in time to come, as I would have tried to do, I have no just cause to grieve."

"What Idol has displaced you?" he rejoined.

"A golden one."

"This is the way the world is! he said. "There is nothing on which it is so hard as poverty. And there is nothing it condemns with such severity as the pursuit of wealth!"

"You fear the world too much," she answered, gently.

"All your other hopes have merged into the hope of being beyond the world's reproach. I have seen your nobler aspirations fall off one by one, until the master-passion, Gain, possesses you. Have I not?"

"What then?" he retorted. "Even if I have grown so much wiser, what then? I am not changed towards you."

She shook her head.

"Am I?"

"Our contract is an old one. It was made when we were both poor and content to be so, until we could improve our worldly fortune by our hard work. You are changed. When our contract was made, you were another man."

"I was a boy," he said impatiently.

"Your own feeling tells you that you were not what you are," she returned. "I am. The engagement that promised happiness when we were one in heart, is filled with misery now that we are two. How often and how keenly I have thought of this, I will not say. It is enough that I have thought of it, and can release you."

"Have I ever sought release?"

"Not in words. No. Never."

"In what, then?"

"In a changed nature, in an altered spirit. In another way of life with another Hope as its great goal. In everything that made my love of any worth or value in your sight. If this had never been between us," said the girl, looking mildly, but with steadiness, upon him, "tell me, would you seek me out and try to win me now? Ah, no!"

He seemed to yield to the justice of this supposition, in spite of himself. But he said, with a struggle, "You think not."

"I would gladly think otherwise if I could," she answered, "Heaven knows! When I have learned a truth like this, I know how strong and irresistible it must be. But if you were free today, tomorrow, yesterday, can even I believe that you would choose a penniless girl—you, who weigh everything by Gain. And if you chose her, if for a moment you were false enough to your one guiding principle to do so, do I not know that your repentance and regret would surely follow? I do, and I release you. With a full heart, for the love of him you once were."

He was about to speak, but with her head turned from him, she resumed.

"You may—the memory of what is past half makes me hope you will—have pain in this. A very, very brief time, and you will dismiss the recollection of it, gladly, as an unprofitable dream, from which it happened well that you awoke. May you be happy in the life you have chosen!"

She left him, and they parted.

"Spirit!" said Scrooge, "Show me no more! Conduct me home. Why do you delight to torture me?"

"One shadow more!" exclaimed the Ghost.

"No more!" cried Scrooge. "No more. I don't wish to see it. Show me no more!"

But the relentless Ghost held him tightly by the arms, and forced him to observe what happened next.

They were in another scene and place. It was a room, not very large or handsome, but full of comfort. Near to the winter fire sat a beautiful young girl, so like the last that Scrooge believed it was the same until he saw her, now a lovely woman, sitting opposite her daughter. The noise in this room was perfectly tumultuous, for there were more children there than Scrooge in his agitated state of mind could count. Every child was making as much noise as forty. The results were uproarious beyond belief, but no one seemed to care. On the contrary, the mother and daughter laughed heartily, and enjoyed it very much. The daughter, soon joining in the nonsense, was tossed about by her brothers quite ruthlessly. What would I not have given to be one of them! Though I never could have been so rude, no, no! I wouldn't for the wealth of all the world have crushed that braided hair, and torn it down. As for the precious little shoe, I wouldn't have plucked it off, God bless my soul! to save my life. As to measuring her waist in sport, as they did, bold young brood, I couldn't have done it. I should have expected my arm to have grown round it for a punishment, and never come straight again. And yet I should have dearly liked, I own, to have touched her lips. I would like to have looked upon the lashes of her downcast eyes, and never raised a blush, to have let loose waves of hair, an inch of which would be a keepsake beyond price. In short, I should have liked, I do confess, to have had the lightest license of a child, and yet been man enough to know its value.

But now a knocking at the door was heard. The boisterous group, greeted the father, who came home laden with Christmas toys and presents. then the shouting and the struggling, and the onslaught that was made on the defenceless fellow! They dove into his pockets, took his brown-paper parcels, held on tight by his cravat, hugged him round the neck, pommelled his back, and kicked his legs in irrepressible affection! the shouts of wonder and delight with which the opening of every package was received! The terrible announcement that the baby had been caught in the act of putting a doll's frying-pan into his mouth, and was suspected of having swallowed a toy turkey, glued on a wooden platter!

The immense relief of finding this a false alarm! The joy, and gratitude, and ecstasy! They are all indescribable alike. It is enough that by degrees the children and their emotions got out of the parlour and by one stair at a time, up to the top of the house, where they went to bed, and so subsided.

And now Scrooge looked on more attentively than ever, when the master of the house sat down with his daughter and her mother at his own fireside. When Scrooge thought that such a child might have called him father, and been a springtime in the haggard winter of his life, his sight grew very dim indeed.

"Belle," said the husband, turning to his wife with a smile, "I saw an old friend of yours this afternoon."

"Who was it?"

"Guess!"

"How can I? Tut, don't I know," she added in the same breath, laughing as he laughed. "Mr. Scrooge."

"Mr. Scrooge it was. I passed his office window. As it was not shut up, and he had a candle inside, I could scarcely help seeing him. His partner lies upon the point of death, I hear. And there he sat alone. Quite alone in the world, I do believe."

"Spirit!" said Scrooge in a broken voice, "remove me from this place."

"I told you these were shadows of the things that have been," said the Ghost. "That they are what they are, do not blame me!"

"Remove me!" Scrooge exclaimed. "I cannot bear it!"

He turned upon the Ghost. Seeing that it

looked upon him with a face, in which in some strange way there were fragments of all the faces it had shown him, wrestled with it.

"Leave me! Take me back. Haunt me no longer!"

In the struggle, if it can be called a struggle, since the Ghost undisturbed by it, Scrooge observed that its light was burning high and bright. Dimly connecting that with its power over him, he seized the extinguisher-cap, and pressed it down upon its head.

The Spirit dropped beneath it, so that the extinguisher covered its whole form. But though Scrooge pressed it down with all his force, he could not hide the light. Brightness streamed from under it, in an unbroken flood upon the ground.

He was conscious of being exhausted, and overcome by an irresistible drowsiness. He was also aware of being in his own bedroom. He gave the cap a parting squeeze, in which his hand relaxed, and had barely time to reel to bed before he sank into a heavy sleep.

STAVE THREE.

THE SECOND OF THE THREE SPIRITS.

Scrooge awoke in the middle of a loud snore, and sat up in bed to get his thoughts together. No one had to tell him that the bell was again striking one. He felt that he was awakened for the special purpose of meeting the second messenger sent to him through Jacob Marley's intervention. But finding that he turned uncomfortably cold when he began to wonder which of his curtains this new spectre would draw back, he pulled them all aside with his own hands. Lying down again, he watched sharply all round the bed. For he wished to challenge the Spirit the minute it appeared. He did not wish to be taken by surprise and made nervous.

I don't mind asking you to believe that Scrooge was ready for a wide variety of strange appearances. Nothing between a baby and a rhinoceros would have astonished him very much.

Now, being prepared for almost anything, he was not by any means prepared for nothing. Consequently, when the bell struck one, and no shape appeared, he was taken with a violent fit of trembling. Five minutes, ten minutes, a quarter of an hour went by, yet nothing came. All this time he lay upon his bed. He was at the center of a bright light, which shone upon the bed when the clock struck the hour. Since this was the only light, it was more alarming than a dozen ghosts. Scrooge was powerless to figure out what it meant, what it would do. He was sometimes afraid that he might be at that very moment an interesting case of spontaneous combustion. At last he began to think that the source of this ghostly light might be in the next room. Having decided this was so, he got up softly and shuffled in his slippers to the door.

The moment Scrooge's hand was on the lock, a strange voice called him by his name and told him to enter. He obeyed.

It was his own room. There was no doubt about that. But it had undergone a surprising transformation. The walls and ceiling were so hung with green leaves, that it looked like a grove. Bright gleaming berries glistened from every part of it. The crisp leaves of holly, mistletoe, and ivy reflected back the light, as if so many little mirrors had been scattered there. Such a mighty blaze went roaring up the chimney, as that dull hearth had never known in Scrooge's time, or Marley's, or for many a winter season gone. Heaped up upon the floor, to form a kind of throne, were turkeys, geese, game, poultry, brawn, great joints of meat, suckling pigs, long wreaths of sausages, mince-pies, plum-puddings, barrels of oysters, red-hot chestnuts, cherry-cheeked apples, juicy oranges, luscious pears, immense twelfthcakes, and seething bowls of punch that made the chamber dim with their delicious steam. Upon this couch there sat a jolly giant, glorious to see. He bore a glowing torch,

shaped like a horn of plenty, and held it up to shed its light on Scrooge, as he came peeping round the door.

"Come in!" exclaimed the Ghost. "Come in! and know me better, man!"

Scrooge entered timidly, and hung his head before this spirit. He was not the dogged Scrooge he had been. And though the spirit's eyes were clear and kind, he did not like to meet them.

"I am the Ghost of Christmas Present," said the Spirit. "Look upon me!"

Scrooge reverently did so. The Ghost was clothed in one simple deep green robe, or mantle, bordered with white fur. This garment hung loosely on the figure. Its feet, observable beneath the ample folds of the garment, were bare. On its head it wore a holly wreath set here and there with shining icicles. Its dark brown curls were long and free—free as its genial face, its sparkling eye, its open hand, its cheery voice, its open manner, and its joyful air. Fastened round its middle was an antique scabbard. But no sword was in it, and the ancient sheath was eaten up with rust.

"You have never seen the like of me before!" exclaimed the Spirit.

"Never," Scrooge answered.

"You never walked forth with the younger members of my family, meaning (for I am very young) my elder brothers born in these later years?" pursued the Phantom.

"I don't think I have," said Scrooge. "I am afraid I have not. Have you had many brothers, Spirit?"

"More than eighteen hundred," said the Ghost.

"A tremendous family to provide for!" muttered Scrooge.

The Ghost of Christmas Present rose.

"Spirit," said Scrooge submissively, "take me where you will. I went forth last night because I was forced to, and I learned a lesson which is working now. Tonight, if you have anything to teach me, let me profit by it."

"Touch my robe!"

Scrooge did as he was told, and held it tight.

Holly, mistletoe, red berries, ivy, turkeys, geese, game, poultry, brawn, meat, pigs, sausages, oysters, pies, puddings, fruit, and punch, all vanished instantly. So did the room, the fire, the bright light, and the hour of night. They stood in the city streets on Christmas morning. The weather was severe, and the people made a rough, but brisk and pleasant kind of music, in scraping the snow from the pavement in front of their houses.

The house fronts looked black enough, and the windows blacker, contrasting with the smooth white sheet of snow upon the roofs. The snow had been plowed up in deep furrows by the heavy wheels of carts and wagons. The furrows were hard to trace in the thick yellow mud and icy water. The sky was gloomy, and the shortest streets were choked up with a dingy mist filled with particles of soot. It was as if all the chimneys in Great Britain were blazing away to their hearts' content. There was nothing very cheerful in the climate or the town, and yet there was an air of cheerfulness that the clearest summer air and brightest summer sun could not have produced.

For the people who were shovelling snow from

their walks and housetops were jovial and full of glee. They called out to one another from the parapets. Now and then they exchanged snowballs—laughing heartily if they went right, and not less heartily if they went wrong. The poulterers' shops were still open, and the fruiterers' were radiant in their glory. There were great, round, pot-bellied baskets of chestnuts, shaped like the waistcoats of jolly old gentlemen, standing at the doors. There were large, ruddy, brown Spanish onions, shining in the fatness of their growth. There were pears and apples, clustered high in blooming pyramids. There were bunches of grapes dangling from hooks. There were piles of filberts, mossy and brown, recalling, in their fragrance, ancient walks in the woods. The very gold and silver fish, set forth among these choice fruits in a bowl, appeared to know that there was something going on.

The grocers! Oh the grocers! nearly closed, with perhaps two shutters down, or one. It was not just that the scales on the counter made a merry sound, or that the blended scents of tea and coffee were so pleasant to the nose, or even that the raisins were so plentiful and rare, the almonds so extremely white, the sticks of cinnamon so long and straight, the other spices so delicious, the candied fruits so caked and spotted with molten sugar as to make the coldest onlookers feel faint. Nor was it that the figs were moist and pulpy, or that the French plums blushed in their highly decorated boxes, or that everything was good to eat and in its Christmas dress. But the customers were all so hurried and so eager in the hopeful promise of the day, that they tumbled up against each other at the door, clashing their wicker baskets wildly, and left their purchases upon the counter, and came running back to fetch them, and committed hundreds of similar mistakes in the best humor possible. The grocer and his people were so pleasant and cheerful that the polished hearts with which they fastened their aprons might have been their own.

But soon the bells in the steeples called people to church and chapel, and away they came, flocking through the streets in their best clothes, and with their happiest faces. At the same time there came from the little side streets, lanes, and nameless turnings, innumerable people, carrying their dinners to the bakers' shops. The sight of these poor revellers appeared to interest the spirit very much, for he stood with Scrooge beside him in a baker's doorway. Taking off the pot covers as the people passed, the spirit sprinkled incense on their dinners from his torch. It was a very uncommon kind of torch, for once or twice when there were angry words between some dinner carriers who had bumped into each other, he shed a few drops of water on them from it, and their good humor was restored immediately. For they said it was a shame to quarrel upon Christmas Day. And so it was! God love it, so it was!

In time the bells ceased, and the bakers' were shut up. Yet there was a joyful foreshadowing of all these dinners in the thawed snow above each baker's oven.

"Is there a peculiar flavor in what you sprinkle from your torch?" asked Scrooge.

"There is. My own."

"Would it apply to any kind of dinner on this day?" asked Scrooge.

"To any kindly given. To a poor one most."

"Why to a poor one most?" asked Scrooge.

"Because it needs it most."

"Spirit," said Scrooge, after a moment's thought, "I am surprised that you, of all the beings, should desire to limit these people's opportunities for innocent enjoyment."

"I!" cried the Spirit.

"You would deprive them of their means of dining every seventh day, often the only day on which they can be said to dine at all," said Scrooge. "Wouldn't you?"

"I!" cried the spirit.

"You seek to close these bakers' shops on Sundays," said Scrooge. "And it comes to the same thing."

"I see!" exclaimed the spirit.

"Forgive me if I am wrong. It has been done in your name, or at least in that of your family," said Scrooge.

"There are some upon this earth of yours," returned the Spirit, "who claim to know us, and who do their deeds of passion, pride, ill will, hatred, envy, bigotry, and selfishness in our name. They are as strange to us and all our kith and kin, as if they had never lived. Remember that, and blame their doings on themselves, not us."

Scrooge promised that he would. They went on, invisible, as they had been before, into the suburbs of the town. It was a remarkable quality of the Ghost (which Scrooge had observed at the baker's) that in spite of his gigantic size, he could fit into any place with ease. He stood beneath a low roof quite as gracefully as he could have done in any lofty hall.

And perhaps it was the pleasure the good Spirit had in showing off this power of his, or else it was his own kind, generous, hearty nature, and his sympathy with all poor men, that led him straight to Scrooge's clerk's house. For there he went, and took Scrooge with him, holding to his robe. On the threshold of the door the spirit smiled, and stopped to bless Bob Cratchit's dwelling with the sprinklings of his torch. Think of that! Bob had but fifteen "Bob" a week himself. Yet the Ghost of Christmas Present blessed his four-roomed house!

Then up rose Mrs. Cratchit, Cratchit's wife, dressed poorly in an old gown, but wearing bright ribbons, which are cheap and make a goodly show for sixpence. She laid the cloth on the table, assisted by Belinda Cratchit, second of her daughters, also wearing ribbons. Master Peter Cratchit plunged a fork into the saucepan of potatoes. He was wearing one of his father's large shirt collars, and yearned to show off his grown-up attire in the fashionable Parks. And now two smaller Cratchits, boy and girl, came tearing in, screaming that outside the baker's they had smelt the goose, and recognized it as their own. Thinking luxurious thoughts about sage and onion stuffing, these young Cratchits danced about the table, and praised Master Peter Cratchit to the skies. He (not proud, although his collars nearly choked him) blew on the fire, until the potatoes knocked loudly at the saucepan lid to be let out and peeled.

"Where is your dear father then?" said Mrs. Cratchit. "And your brother, Tiny Tim. And Martha wasn't nearly as late last Christmas Day!" "Here's Martha, Mother!" said a girl, appearing as she spoke.

"Here's Martha, Mother!" cried the two young Cratchits. "Hurrah! There's such a goose, Martha!"

"Why, bless your heart alive, my dear, how late you are!" said Mrs. Cratchit, kissing her a dozen times, and taking off her shawl and bonnet for her. "We had a lot of work to finish up last night," replied the girl, "and had to clear away this morning, Mother!"

"Well! Never mind so long as you are come," said Mrs. Cratchit. "Sit down before the fire, my dear, and warm yourself, Lord bless you!"

"No no! There's Father coming," cried the two young Cratchits, who were everywhere at once. "Hide, Martha, hide!"

So Martha hid herself, and in came Bob, the father, with at least three feet of muffler, not counting the fringe, hanging down before him. His threadbare clothes were darned up and brushed. Tiny Tim sat upon his shoulder. Alas for Tiny Tim, he carried a little crutch, and had his legs encased in an iron brace!

"Why, where's our Martha?" cried Bob Cratchit looking round.

"Not coming," said Mrs. Cratchit.

"Not coming!" said Bob, with a sudden lowering his high spirits. For he had been Tim's horse all the way from church, and had come home galloping. "Not coming upon Christmas Day!"

Martha didn't like to see him disappointed,

even if it were only a joke. So she came out from behind the closet door, and ran into his arms. The two young Cratchits took Tiny Tim into the wash-house so that he could hear the pudding singing in the copper pot.

"And how did little Tim behave?" asked Mrs. Cratchit, when Bob had hugged his daughter to his heart's content.

"As good as gold," said Bob, "and better. Somehow he gets thoughtful sitting by himself so much, and thinks the strangest things you ever heard. He told me, coming home, that he hoped the people saw him in the church, because he was a cripple. He thought it might be pleasant for them to remember on Christmas Day, who made lame beggars walk and blind men see."

Bob's voice shook when he told them this, and trembled more when he said that Tiny Tim was growing strong and hearty.

An active little crutch was heard upon the floor. Back came Tiny Tim before another word was spoken, escorted by his brother and sister to his stool beside the fire. And Bob, turning up his shabby cuffs, made some punch and stirred it round and round and put it on the hob to simmer. Master Peter and the two ubiquitous young Cratchits went to fetch the goose from the baker's. They soon returned, carrying the roast goose with great dignity.

Such excitement followed that you might have thought a goose the rarest of all birds. It seemed like a miracle with feathers, and in truth it was something very like it in that house. Mrs. Cratchit made the gravy (ready beforehand in a little saucepan) hissing hot. Master Peter mashed the potatoes with incredible vigor. Miss Belinda sweetened up the applesauce. Martha served the hot plates. Bob took Tiny Tim beside him in a tiny corner at the table. The two young Cratchits set chairs for everybody, not forgetting themselves. At last the dishes were set on the table, and grace was said. It was followed by a breathless pause, as Mrs. Cratchit, prepared to carve the goose's breast. When she did, and when the long expected gush of stuffing came forth, one murmur of delight arose all round the table. Even Tiny Tim, beat on the table with the handle of his knife, and feebly cried, "Hurrah!"

There never was such a goose. Bob said he didn't believe there ever was such a goose cooked. Its tenderness and flavor, size and cheapness, were the themes of universal admiration. With the applesauce and mashed potatoes, it was enough dinner for the whole family. Indeed, as Mrs. Cratchit said with great delight (looking at a tiny bone left on the dish), they hadn't eaten it all yet! But every one had enough, and the youngest Cratchits in particular, were up to their ears in sage and onion stuffing! But now, the plates being changed by Miss Belinda, Mrs. Cratchit left the room to bring the pudding in.

Suppose it should not be done enough! Suppose it should break in turning out! Suppose somebody should have got over the wall of the backyard and stolen it, while they were eating the goose! All sorts of horrors were supposed.

Hallo! A great deal of steam! The pudding was out of the copper pot. A smell like washing day!

That was the cloth. A smell like an eating house, and a pastry cook's next door to each other, with a laundress's next door to that! That was the pudding. In half a minute Mrs. Cratchit entered. She was smiling proudly. She brought the pudding so hard and firm, blazing in ignited brandy, and decorated with Christmas holly stuck into the top.

Oh, a wonderful pudding! Bob Cratchit said that he regarded it as the greatest success achieved by Mrs. Cratchit since their marriage. Mrs. Cratchit said that now that the weight was off her mind, she would confess she had her doubts about the quantity of flour. Everybody had something to say about it, but nobody said or thought it was at all a small pudding for a large family. It would have been awful to do so. Any Cratchit would have blushed to hint at such a thing.

At last the dinner was all done, the table was cleared, the hearth swept, and the fire made up. The punch was tasted and considered perfect. Apples and oranges were put on the table. A shovelful of chestnuts were put on the fire. Then all the Cratchit family drew round the hearth. At Bob Cratchit's elbow stood the family's glasses. There were two tumblers and a cup without a handle.

These held the hot punch from the jug as well as golden goblets would have done. Bob served it out with beaming looks, while the chestnuts on the fire sputtered and crackled noisily. Then Bob said:

"A Merry Christmas to us all, my dears. God bless us!"

Which all the family re-echoed.

"God bless us every one!" said Tiny Tim, the last of all.

He sat very close to his father's side on his little stool. Bob held Tim's little hand in his, as if he wished to keep him by his side, and dreaded that he might be taken from him.

"Spirit," said Scrooge, with an interest he had never felt before, "tell me if Tiny Tim will live."

"I see a vacant seat," replied the Ghost, "in the poor chimney corner, and a crutch without an owner, carefully preserved. If these shadows remain unchanged by the Future, the child will die."

"No, no," said Scrooge. "Oh no, kind Spirit! Say he will be spared."

"If these shadows remain unchanged by the Future, none other of my race," replied the Ghost, "will find him here. What then? If he is like to die, he had better do it, and decrease the surplus population."

Scrooge hung his head to hear his own words quoted by the Spirit, and was overcome with penitence and grief.

"Man," said the Ghost, "if man you are in your heart, give up that wicked talk until you have discovered what the surplus is, and where it is. Will you decide what men shall live, what men shall die? It may be, that in the sight of Heaven, you are more worthless and less fit to live than millions like this poor man's child. Oh God! To hear the insect on the leaf talking about too much life among his hungry brothers in the dust!"

Scrooge bent before the Ghost's rebuke, and cast his eyes upon the ground. But he raised them speedily, on hearing his own name.

"Mr. Scrooge!" said Bob. "I'll give you Mr. Scrooge, the Founder of the Feast!"

"The Founder of the Feast indeed!" cried Mrs. Cratchit, getting red in the face. "I wish I had him here. I'd give him a piece of my mind to feast upon, and I hope he'd have a good appetite for it."

"My dear," said Bob, "the children! Christmas Day."

"It should be Christmas Day, I am sure," said she, "on which one drinks the health of such an awful, stingy, hard, unfeeling man as Mr. Scrooge. You know he is, Robert! Nobody knows it better than you do, poor fellow!"

"My dear," was Bob's mild answer, "Christmas Day."

"I'll drink his health for your sake and the day's," said Mrs. Cratchit, "not for his. Long life to him! A merry Christmas and a happy New Year! He'll be very merry and very happy, I have no doubt!"

The children drank the toast after her. It was the first of their proceedings which had no heartiness in it. Tiny Tim drank it last of all, but he didn't care about it. Scrooge was the ogre of the family. The mention of his name cast a dark shadow on the party that lasted for a full five minutes.

After it had passed away, they were ten times merrier than before, from the mere relief of Scrooge the Evil being done with. Bob Cratchit told them how he had found a job for Master Peter which would bring in five-and-sixpence weekly. The two young Cratchits laughed tremendously at the idea of Peter's being a man of business. Peter himself looked thoughtfully at the fire from between his collars, as if he were thinking of what he would spend all that money on. Martha, who was a poor apprentice at a hat maker's, then told them what kind of work she had to do, and how many hours she worked at a stretch, and how she meant to lie in bed tomorrow morning for a good long rest. Tomorrow was a holiday she could spend at home. She also told them that she had seen a countess and a lord some days before. She said that the lord "was about as tall as Peter." Hearing this, Peter pulled up his collars so high that you couldn't have seen his head if you had been there. All this time the chestnuts and the punch went round and round. Bye and bye they had a song, about a lost child travelling in the snow, from Tiny Tim He had a plaintive little voice, and sang it very well indeed.

There was nothing special about this. They were not a handsome family. They were not well dressed. Their shoes were badly made. Their clothes were shabby. But they were happy, grateful, and pleased with one another. When they faded, and looked happier yet in the bright sprinklings of the Spirit's torch at parting, Scrooge had his eye upon them, and especially on Tiny Tim, until the last.

By this time it was getting dark, and snowing pretty heavily. As Scrooge and the Spirit went along the streets, the brightness of the roaring fires in kitchens, parlors, and all sorts of rooms, was wonderful. Here, the flickering of the blaze showed preparations for a cosy dinner, with hot plates baking through and through before the fire, and deep red curtains, ready to be drawn, to shut out cold and darkness. There, all the children of the house were running out into the snow to meet their married sisters, brothers, cousins, uncles, aunts, and be the first to greet them. Here, again, were shadows on the window shades of guests assembling. There a group of handsome girls, all hooded and fur-booted, and all chattering at once, tripped lightly off to some near neighbor's house.

But if you had judged from the numbers of people on their way to friendly gatherings, you might have thought that no one was at home to give them welcome when they got there. But every house expected company, and piled up its fires half-chimney high. Blessings on it, how the Ghost exulted! How it floated on, outpouring, with a generous hand, its bright and harmless mirth on everything within its reach! The very lamplighter, who ran on before dotting the dusky street with specks of light, and who was dressed to spend the evening somewhere, laughed out loudly as the Spirit passed. Little did the lamplighter know that he had any company but Christmas!

And now, without a word of warning from the Ghost, they stood upon a bleak and desert moor, where monstrous masses of rude stone were cast about, as though it were the burial place of giants. Water spread itself all over. Frost held it prisoner. Nothing grew but moss and furze, and coarse, rank grass. Down in the west the setting sun had left a streak of fiery red, which glared upon the desolation for an instant, like a sullen eye, and frowning lower, lower, lower yet, was lost in the thick gloom of darkest night.

"What place is this?" asked Scrooge.

"A place where miners live, who labor in the

bowels of the earth," returned the Spirit. "But they know me. See!"

A light shone from the window of a hut, and swiftly they advanced towards it. Passing through the wall of mud and stone, they found a cheerful group assembled round a glowing fire. An old, old man and woman, with their children and their children's children, and another generation beyond that, all dressed in their holiday attire. The old man, in a voice that seldom rose above the howling of the wind on the moor, was singing them a Christmas song. It had been a very old song when he was a boy. From time to time they all joined in the chorus. As soon as they raised their voices, the old man got quite loud. As soon as they stopped, his voice sank again.

The Spirit did not stay here long, but told Scrooge to hold his robe, and passing on above the moor, sped where? Not to sea? To sea. To Scrooge's horror, looking back, he saw the last of the land, a frightful range of rocks, behind them. His ears were deafened by the thundering of water, as it rolled, and roared, and raged among the dreadful caverns it had worn, and fiercely tried to undermine the earth.

Built upon a dismal reef of sunken rocks, some mile or so from shore, on which the waters dashed all year through, there stood a solitary lighthouse. Great heaps of seaweed clung to its base, and storm birds rose and fell about it, like the waves they skimmed.

But even here, two men who watched the light had made a fire, that shed a ray of brightness on the awful sea. Shaking hands over the rough table at which they sat, they wished each other Merry Christmas. One of them sang a sturdy song that was like a gale in itself.

Again the Ghost sped on above the sea until, being far away, as he told Scrooge, from any shore, they landed on a ship. They stood beside the helmsman at the wheel, the lookout in the bow, the officers who had the watch. They were dark, ghostly figures, but every man among them hummed a Christmas tune, or had a Christmas thought, or spoke to his companion of some bygone Christmas Day, with homeward hopes belonging to it. And every man on board, waking or sleeping, good or bad, had had a kinder word for another on that day than on any day in the year. And he had shared to some extent in its festivities, and had remembered those he cared for at a distance, and had known that they delighted to remember him.

It was a great surprise to Scrooge to hear a hearty laugh. It was a much greater surprise to Scrooge to recognize it as his own nephew's, and to find himself in a bright, dry, gleaming room, with the spirit standing smiling by his side, and looking at that same nephew with warm approval!

"Ha, ha!" laughed Scrooge's nephew. "Ha, ha, ha!"

If you should happen, by any unlikely chance, to know a man more blest in a laugh than Scrooge's nephew, all I can say is, I should like to know him too. Introduce him to me. I would like to know him.

There is nothing in the world so contagious as laughter and good humor. When Scrooge's nephew laughed in this way, his wife laughed as heartily as he. And their assembled friends laughed as happily as they did.

"Ha, ha! Ha, ha, ha, ha!"

"He said that Christmas was a humbug, as I live!" cried Scrooge's nephew. "He believed it too!"

"More shame for him, Fred!" said his wife indignantly. Bless those women. They never do anything halfheartedly. They are always in earnest.

She was very pretty. She had a dimpled, surprised-looking face, a ripe little mouth that seemed made to be kissed, and the sunniest pair of eyes you ever saw. Altogether she was perfectly delightful!

"He's a comical old fellow," said Scrooge's nephew, "that's the truth—and not so pleasant as he might be. However, his offenses carry their own punishment, and I have nothing to say against him."

"I'm sure he is very rich, Fred," hinted his wife. "At least you always tell me so."

"What of that, my dear!" said Scrooge's nephew. "His wealth is of no use to him. He doesn't do any good with it. He doesn't make himself comfortable with it. He hasn't the satisfaction of thinking—ha, ha, ha!—that he is ever going to benefit us with it."

"I have no patience with him," observed his wife. Her sisters and all the other ladies expressed the same opinion.

"Oh, I have!" said Scrooge's nephew. "I am sorry for him. I couldn't be angry with him if I tried. Who suffers by his ill whims? Himself, always. Here, he takes it into his head to dislike us, and he won't come and dine with us. What's the result? He doesn't lose much of a dinner."

"Indeed, I think he loses a very good dinner," interrupted his wife. Everybody else said the same, and they must be allowed to have been competent judges, because they had just had dinner. And, with the dessert upon the table, they clustered round the fire, by lamplight.

"Well! I am very glad to hear it," said Scrooge's nephew, "because I haven't any great faith in these young housekeepers. What do you say, Topper?"

Topper had clearly got his eye upon one of the ladies, for he answered that a bachelor was a wretched outcast who had no right to express an opinion on the subject. At this, one of the ladies blushed.

"Do go on, Fred," said Scrooge's niece-in-law, clapping her hands. "He never finishes what he begins to say! He is such a ridiculous fellow!"

Scrooge's nephew laughed again. Everyone joined him merrily.

"I was only going to say," said Scrooge's nephew, "that the consequence of his taking a dislike to us, and not making merry with us, is, as I think, that he loses some pleasant moments, which could do him no harm. I am sure he loses pleasanter companions than he can find in his own thoughts, either in his moldy old office, or his dusty chambers. I mean to give him the same chance every year, whether he likes it or not, for I pity him. He may complain about Christmas till he dies, but he can't help thinking better of it if he finds me going there year after year and saying Uncle Scrooge, how are you? If it only causes him to leave his poor clerk fifty pounds, that's something. And I think I shook him, yesterday."

It was their turn to laugh now, at the notion of his shaking Scrooge. But being thoroughly good-natured, and not much caring what they laughed at, he encouraged them in their merriment.

After tea, they had some music. For they were a musical family. Scrooge's niece-in-law played well upon the harp. She played among other tunes a simple little song that was the favorite of the child who fetched Scrooge from the boarding school, as he had been reminded by the Ghost of Christmas Past. When this strain of music sounded, all the things that Ghost had shown him, came to his mind. He softened more and more. He thought that if he could have listened to it often, years ago, he might have created his own happiness with his own hands, without resorting to the methods that buried Jacob Marley.

But they didn't devote the whole evening to music. After a while they played some children's games. For it is good to be children sometimes, and never better than at Christmas, when its mighty Founder was a child himself.

Scrooge's niece-in-law sat with a large chair and a footstool, in a snug corner, where the Ghost and Scrooge were close behind her. There might have been twenty people there, young and old, but they all played, and so did Scrooge. For, wholly forgetting that his voice made no sound in their ears, he sometimes came out with his guess quite loud, and very often guessed right, too.

The Ghost was greatly pleased to find him in this mood, and looked upon him with such favor that Scrooge begged like a boy to be allowed to stay until the guests departed. But this the Spirit said could not be done.

"Here's a new game," said Scrooge. "One half hour, Spirit, only one!"

It was a Game called Yes and No, where Scrooge's nephew had to think of something, and the rest must find out what. He only answered to their questions yes or no as the case was. The brisk fire of questioning elicited from him that he was thinking of an animal. It was a live animal. It was rather a disagreeable animal. It was a savage animal, an animal that growled and grunted sometimes, and talked sometimes. It lived in London, and walked about the streets. It wasn't made a show of, and wasn't led by anybody, and didn't live in a menagerie, and was never killed in a market. It was not a horse, or a cow, or a bull, or a tiger, or a dog, or a pig, or a cat, or a bear. At every fresh question that was put to him, this nephew burst into a fresh roar of laughter. At last the pretty young lady, his sister-in-law, cried out:

"I have found it out! I know what it is, Fred! I know what it is!"

"What is it?" cried Fred.

"It's your Uncle Scro-o-o-oge!"

Which it certainly was. Some objected that the reply to "Is it a bear?" ought to have been "Yes." They said that an answer of "No" was sufficient to have diverted their thoughts from Mr. Scrooge, supposing they had ever had any tendency that way.

"He has given us plenty of merriment, I am sure," said Fred, "and it would be ungrateful not to drink his health. Here is a glass of mulled wine ready to our hand at the moment. I say 'Uncle

Scrooge!'"

"Well! Uncle Scrooge!" they cried.

"A Merry Christmas and a Happy New Year to the old man, whatever he is!" said Scrooge's nephew. "He wouldn't take it from me, but may he have it, nevertheless. Uncle Scrooge!"

Uncle Scrooge had become so light of heart that he would have toasted them in return if the Ghost had given him time. But the whole scene passed off in the breath of the last word spoken by his nephew. He and the Spirit were again upon their travels.

Much they saw, and far they went, and many homes they visited, but always with a happy end. The Spirit stood beside sick beds, and they were cheerful. It stood by struggling men, and they were patient in their greater hope. It stood by poverty, and it was rich. In almshouse, hospital, and jail, in misery's every refuge, where vain man had not barred the Spirit out, he left his blessing, and taught Scrooge his precepts.

It was a long night, if it were only a night. But Scrooge had doubted this, because the Christmas Holidays appeared to be condensed into the space of time they spent together. It was strange, too, that while Scrooge remained unchanged in his outward form, the Ghost grew older, clearly older. Scrooge had observed this change, but never spoke of it, until they left a children's Twelfth Night party. Looking at the Spirit as they stood together in an open place, he noticed that its hair was gray. "Are spirits' lives so short?" asked Scrooge.

"My life upon this globe is very brief," replied the Ghost. "It ends tonight."

"Tonight!" cried Scrooge.

"Tonight at midnight. Hark! The time is drawing near."

The chimes were ringing the three quarters past eleven at that moment.

"Forgive me if I am not justified in what I ask," said Scrooge, looking intently at the Spirit's robe, "but I see something strange, and not belonging to yourself, protruding from your skirts. Is it a foot or a claw?"

"It might be a claw, for there is little flesh upon it," was the Spirit's sorrowful reply. "Look here."

From the foldings of its robe, it brought two children. They were wretched, abject, frightful, hideous, miserable. They knelt down at its feet, and clung to the outside of its garment.

"Oh, Man! Look here. Look, look, down here!" exclaimed the Ghost.

They were a boy and girl. Yellow, meager, ragged, scowling, wolfish. But they were prostrate, too, in their humility. Where graceful youth should have filled their features out, and touched them with its freshest tints, a stale and shrivelled hand, like that of age, had pinched and twisted them, and pulled them into shreds. Where angels might have sat enthroned, devils lurked, and glared out menacing. No change, no degradation, no perversion of humanity, in any grade, through all the mysteries of wonderful creation, has monsters half so horrible and dread.

Scrooge shrank back, appalled. He tried to say they were fine children, but the words choked themselves.

"Spirit! Are they yours?" Scrooge could say no more.

"They are Man's," said the Spirit, looking down upon them. "And they cling to me. This boy is Ignorance. This girl is Want. Beware them both, but most of all beware this boy, for on his brow I see that Doom is written, unless the writing is erased. Deny it!" cried the Spirit, stretching out its hand towards the city. "Slander those who tell it to you! Admit it for your own purposes, and make it worse! And await the end!"

"Have they no refuge or resource?" cried Scrooge.

"Are there no prisons?" said the Spirit, turning on him for the last time with his own words. "Are there no workhouses?"

The bell struck twelve.

Scrooge looked about him for the Ghost, and saw it not. As the last stroke ceased to vibrate, he remembered the prediction of old Jacob Marley. Lifting up his eyes, he saw a solemn phantom, draped and hooded, coming, like a mist along the ground, towards him.

STAVE FOUR.

THE LAST OF THE SPIRITS.

THE Phantom slowly, gravely, silently, approached. When it came near him, Scrooge knelt down. For this spirit seemed to scatter gloom and mystery through the very air in which it moved.

It was shrouded in a deep black garment which concealed its head, its face, its form, and left nothing of it visible except one outstretched hand. But for this hand it would have been difficult to separate the Spirit from the darkness that surrounded it.

Scrooge felt that it was tall and stately when it stood beside him. Its mysterious presence filled him with a solemn dread. He knew no more, for the Spirit neither spoke nor moved.

"I am in the presence of the Ghost of Christmas Yet to Come?" said Scrooge.

The Spirit did not answer, but pointed downward with its hand.

"You are about to show me things that have not happened, but will happen in the time before us," Scrooge said. "Is that so, Spirit?"

The upper portion of the garment moved, as if the Spirit had nodded its head. That was the only answer Scrooge received.

Although well used to ghostly company by this

time, Scrooge feared the silent shape so much that his legs trembled beneath him. He found that he could hardly stand when he prepared to follow it. The Spirit paused a moment, as if observing his condition, and giving him time to recover.

But Scrooge was all the worse for this. It thrilled him with a vague uncertain horror, to know that behind the dark shroud there were ghostly eyes intently fixed upon him. He, on the other hand, though he strained to see, could not make out anything but a spectral hand and one great heap of black.

"Ghost of the Future!" Scrooge exclaimed, "I fear you more than any spectre I have seen. But, as I know your purpose is to do me good, and as I hope to live to be another man from what I was, I am prepared to go with you, and do it with a thankful heart. Will you not speak to me?"

It gave him no reply. The hand was pointed straight before them.

"Lead on!" said Scrooge. "Lead on! The night is waning fast, and it is precious time to me, I know. Lead on, Spirit!"

The Phantom moved away as it had come towards him. Scrooge followed in the shadow of its gown, which bore him up, he thought, and carried him along.

They scarcely seemed to enter the city. The city rather seemed to spring up around them. But there they were, in the heart of it. They were there amongst the merchants, who hurried up and down and chinked the money in their pockets, as Scrooge had seen them often do.

The Spirit stopped beside one little group of

businessmen. Observing that the hand was pointed to them, Scrooge advanced to listen to their talk.

"No," said a great fat man with a monstrous chin, "I don't know much about it, either way. I only know he's dead."

"When did he die?" inquired another.

"Last night, I believe."

"Why, what was the matter with him?" asked a third, taking a vast quantity of snuff out of a very large snuffbox. "I thought he'd never die."

"God knows," said the first, with a yawn.

"What has he done with his money?" asked a red-faced gentleman.

"I haven't heard," said the man with the large chin, yawning again. "Left it to his company, perhaps. He hasn't left it to me. That's all I know."

This pleasantry was received with a general laugh.

"It's likely to be a very cheap funeral," said the same speaker, "for upon my life I don't know of anybody to go to it. Suppose we make up a party and volunteer?"

"I don't mind going if a lunch is provided," observed one gentleman. "But I must be fed, if I go to it."

Another laugh.

"Well, I am the most disinterested among you, after all," said the first speaker, "for I never wear signs of mourning, and I never eat lunch. But I'll offer to go, if anybody else will. When I come to think of it, I'm not at all sure that I wasn't his best friend. We used to stop and speak whenever we met. Bye, bye!"

Speakers and listeners strolled away, and

mixed with other groups. Scrooge knew the men, and looked towards the Spirit for an explanation.

The Phantom glided on into a street. Its finger pointed to two persons meeting. Scrooge listened again, thinking that the explanation might lie here.

He knew these men, also, perfectly. They were men of business, very wealthy, and of great importance. He had made a point always of standing well in their esteem. In a business point of view, that is. Strictly in a business point of view.

"How are you?" said one.

"How are you?" returned the other.

"Well!" said the first. "Old Scratch has got his own at last, hey?"

"So I am told," returned the second. "Cold, isn't it?"

"Seasonable for Christmastime. You're not a skater, I suppose?"

"No. No. Something else to think of. Good morning!" Not another word. that was their meeting, their conversation, and their parting.

Scrooge was at first surprised that the Spirit should attach importance to conversations apparently so trivial. But feeling assured that they must have some hidden purpose, he tried to think of what that purpose might be. They could scarcely be supposed to have anything to do with the death of Jacob, his old partner, for that was Past, and this Ghost's time was the Future. Nor could he think of any one he knew to whom he could apply them. But he was sure that these conversations had some lesson for him. He resolved to remember every word he heard, and everything he saw. He would especially observe the shadow of himself when it appeared. For he expected that the conduct of his future self would give him the clue he missed, and would mark the solution of these riddles easy.

He looked about in that very place for his own image. But another man stood in his accustomed corner, and though the clock pointed to his usual time of day for being there, he saw no likeness of himself among the people who came by. It did not surprise him, however. He had been thinking about how he would change his life. He thought and hoped he saw his newborn resolutions carried out in this.

Quiet and dark beside him stood the Phantom, with its outstretched hand. When Scrooge roused himself from thought, he sensed that the unseen eyes were looking at him keenly. It made him shudder, and feel very cold.

They left the busy scene, and went into a part of the town where Scrooge had never been before. He recognized its location, however, and knew its bad reputation. The streets were foul and narrow. The shops and houses were wretched. The people were half-naked, drunken, slipshod, ugly. Alleys and archways, like so many cesspools, discharged their smell, and dirt, and life, upon the streets. The whole neighborhood reeked with crime, with filth, and misery.

In the heart of this part of town there was a shop where iron, old rags, bottles, bones, and greasy offal, were brought. On the floor within were piled up heaps of rusty keys, nails, chains, hinges, files, scales, weights, and used iron of all kinds. Secrets that few would like to know were hidden in mountains of rags, masses of corrupted fat, and sepulchres of bones. Sitting in among the wares he dealt in was a gray-haired man, nearly seventy years of age. He had screened himself from the cold outside air by a curtain of rags hung on a line. He smoked his pipe in all the luxury of calm retirement.

Scrooge and the Phantom came into the presence of this man just as a woman with a heavy bundle slunk into the shop. But she had scarcely entered, when another woman, similarly laden, came in too. And she was closely followed by a man in faded black. All three were started when they recognized one another. After they got over their astonishment, in which the old man with the pipe had joined them, they all three burst into a laugh.

"The charwoman is first!" cried she who had entered first. "The laundress is second and the undertaker's man is third. Look here, old Joe, isn't this something! We all three have all met here without meaning to!"

"You couldn't have met in a better place," said old Joe, removing his pipe from his mouth. "Come into the parlor. You have been welcome here for a long time, you know. The other two aren't strangers either. Wait till I shut the door of the shop. Ah! How it squeaks! There is not rustier bit of metal in the place as its own hinges, I believe. And I'm sure there are no bones here as odd as mine. Ha, ha! We're all suitable to our calling, we're well matched. Come into the parlor. Come into the parlor."

The parlor was the space behind the screen of

rags. The old man raked the fire together with an old stair rod and trimmed his smoky lamp.

While he did this, the woman who had already spoken threw her bundle on the floor and sat down in a flaunting manner on a stool. Crossing her elbows on her knees, she looked with a bold defiance at the other two.

"What odds then! What odds, Mrs. Dilber?" said the woman. "Every person has a right to take care of themselves. He always did!"

"That's true, indeed!" said the laundress. "No man more so."

"Why, then, don't stand staring as if you were afraid, woman. Who's the wiser? We're not going to snitch on each other, are we?"

"No, indeed!" said Mrs. Dilber and the man together. "We should hope not."

"Very well, then!" cried the woman. "That's enough. Who's going to miss a few things like these? Not a dead man, I suppose."

"No, indeed," said Mrs. Dilber, laughing.

"If he wanted to keep them after he was dead, the wicked old thing," pursued the woman, "why wasn't he natural in his lifetime? If he had been, he'd have had somebody to look after him when he was struck with Death, instead of lying gasping out his last there, alone by himself."

"It's the truest word that ever was spoke," said Mrs. Dilber. "It's a judgment on him."

"I wish it was a little heavier one," replied the woman, "and it would have been, you may depend upon it, if I could have laid my hands on anything else. Open that bundle, old Joe, and let me know the value of it. Speak out plain. I'm not afraid to be the first, nor afraid for them to see it. We knew pretty well that we were helping ourselves, before we met here, I believe. It's no sin. Open the bundle, Joe."

But the gallantry of her friends would not allow this. The man in faded black, going first, produced his plunder. It was not much. A seal or two, a pencil case, a pair of sleeve buttons, and a brooch of no great value, were all. They were examined and appraised by old Joe, who wrote what he would pay for each upon the wall. He then added them up into a total when he found that there was nothing more to come.

"That's your account," said Joe, "and I wouldn't give another sixpence, if I was to be boiled for not doing it. Who's next?"

Mrs. Dilber was next. Sheets and towels, some wearing apparel, two old-fashioned silver tea-spoons, a pair of sugar tongs, and a few boots. Her account was stated on the wall in the same manner.

"I always give too much to ladies. It's a weakness of mine, and that's the way I ruin myself," said old Joe. "That's your account. If you asked me for another penny, I'd change my mind and knock off half-a-crown."

"And now undo my bundle, Joe," said the first woman.

Joe went down on his knees and unfastened a great many knots. He dragged out a large and heavy roll of some dark stuff.

"What do you call this?" said Joe. "Bed curtains!"

"Ah!" returned the woman, laughing and

leaning forward on her crossed arms. "Bed curtains!"

"You don't mean to say you took 'em down, rings and all, with him lying there?" said Joe.

"Yes, I do," replied the woman. "Why not?"

"You were born to make your fortune," said Joe, "and you'll certainly do it."

"I certainly won't hesitate to help myself for the sake of such a man as he was, I promise you, Joe," returned the woman coolly. "Don't drop that oil upon the blankets, now."

"His blankets?" asked Joe.

"Whose else's do you think?" replied the woman. "He isn't likely to take cold without them, I dare say."

"I hope he didn't die of anything catching? Eh?" said old Joe, stopping in his work, and looking up.

"Don't you be afraid of that," returned the woman. "I'm not so fond of his company that I'd hang around him, if he did. Ah! You may look through that shirt till your eyes ache. You won't find a hole in it, nor a threadbare place. It's the best he had, and a fine one too. They'd have wasted it, if it hadn't been for me."

"What do you call wasting it?" asked old Joe.

"Putting it on him to be buried in, to be sure," replied the woman with a laugh. "Somebody was fool enough to do it, but I took it off again. If calico isn't good enough for such a purpose, it isn't good enough for anything. It's quite as becoming to the body. He can't look uglier than he did in that one."

Scrooge listened to this dialogue in horror. As the thieves around their loot, Scrooge looked at them with disgust. His feelings could hardly have been greater if they had been selling the corpse itself.

"Ha, ha!" laughed the same woman, when old Joe, producing a flannel bag with money in it, paid each of them. "This is the end of it, you see! He frightened every one away from him when he was alive, to profit us when he was dead! Ha, ha, ha!"

"Spirit!" said Scrooge, shuddering from head to foot. "I see, I see. The case of this unhappy man might be my own. My life tends that way, now. Merciful Heaven, what is this?"

He recoiled in terror, for the scene had changed, and now he almost touched a bed. It was a bare, uncurtained bed. On it, beneath a ragged sheet, there lay a something covered up, which, though it could not speak, announced itself in awful language.

The room was very dark, too dark to be observed with any accuracy. Scrooge glanced round it anxiously, wanting to know what kind of room it was. A pale light fell straight upon the bed. There, unwatched, unwept, uncared for, was the body of this man.

Scrooge glanced towards the Phantom. Its steady hand was pointed to the head. The cover was so carelessly adjusted that the slightest raising of it, the motion of a finger upon Scrooge's part, would have revealed the face. He thought of it, felt how easy it would be to do, and longed to do it. But he had no more power to move the sheet than to dismiss the spectre at his side.

Oh cold, cold, rigid, dreadful Death, set up your altar here, for this is your dominion! But of the loved, revered, and honored dead, you cannot

make one feature ugly. It is not that the hand is heavy and will fall down when released. It is not that the heart and pulse are still. It is that the hand was open, generous, and true. The heart was once brave, warm, and tender, and the pulse was a man's. Strike, Shadow, strike! And see his good deeds springing from the wound, to give the world immortal life!

No voice pronounced these words in Scrooge's ears. Yet he heard them when he looked upon the bed. He thought, if this man could be raised up now, what would be his foremost thoughts? Avarice, hard dealing, griping cares? They have brought him to a rich end, truly!

He lay, in the dark empty house, with not a man, a woman, or a child. He could not say he was kind to me in this or that, and for the memory of one kind word I will be kind to him. A cat was tearing at the door, and there was a sound of gnawing rats beneath the hearth stone. What they wanted in the room of death, and why they were so restless and disturbed, Scrooge did not dare to think.

"Spirit!" he said, "this is a fearful place. In leaving it, I shall not leave its lesson, trust me. Let us go!"

Still the Ghost pointed with an unmoved finger to the head.

"I understand you," Scrooge returned, "and I would do it, if I could. But I have not the power, Spirit. I have not the power."

Again it seemed to look upon him.

"If there is any person in the town, who feels emotion caused by this man's death," said Scrooge quite agonized, "show that person to me, Spirit, I beseech you!"

The Phantom spread its dark robe before him for a moment, like a wing. Withdrawing it, revealed a room by daylight, where a mother and her children were.

She was expecting someone, and with anxious eagerness. She walked up and down the room, started at every sound, looked out from the window, glanced at the clock. She tried, but in vain, to work with her needle. She could hardly bear the voices of the children in their play.

At length the long-expected knock was heard. She hurried to the door, and met her husband. His face was careworn and depressed, though he was young. There was a remarkable expression in it now. It was a kind of serious delight of which he felt ashamed, and which he struggled to repress.

He sat down to the dinner that had been waiting for him by the fire. When she asked him faintly what news he brought, he appeared embarrassed about how to answer.

"Is it good," she said, "or bad?"

"Bad," he answered.

"We are quite ruined?"

"No. There is hope yet, Caroline."

"If he relents," she said, amazed, "there is! Nothing is past hope, if such a miracle has happened."

"He is past relenting," said her husband. "He is dead."

She was a mild and patient woman, but she was thankful in her soul to hear it, and she said so, with clasped hands. She prayed forgiveness the next moment, and was sorry. But her first words were the emotion of her heart.

"What the half-drunken woman whom I told you of last night, said to me, when I tried to see him and obtain a week's delay, and what I thought was a mere excuse to avoid me, turns out to have been quite true. He was not only very ill, but dying, then."

"To whom will our debt be transferred?"

"I don't know. But before that time we shall be ready with the money. Even if we were not, we would be unlikely to find so merciless a creditor in his successor. We may sleep tonight with light hearts, Caroline!"

Yes. Soften it as they would, their hearts were lighter. The children's faces hushed, and clustered round to hear what they so little understood, were brighter. It was a happier house for this man's death! The only emotion that the Ghost could show him, caused by the event, was one of pleasure.

"Let me see some tenderness connected with a death," said Scrooge, "or that dark chamber, Spirit, which we left just now, will be for ever present to me."

The Ghost conducted him through several streets familiar to Scrooge's feet. As they went along, Scrooge looked here and there to find himself, but nowhere was he to be seen. They entered poor Bob Cratchit's house, the dwelling he had visited before. They found the mother and the children seated round the fire.

Quiet. Very quiet. The noisy little Cratchits were as still as statues in one corner, and sat looking up at Peter, who had a book before him. The mother and her daughters were engaged in sewing. But surely they were very quiet!

"'And He took a child, and set him in the midst of them.'"

Where had Scrooge heard those words? He had not dreamed them. The boy must have read them out, as he and the Spirit crossed the threshold. Why did he not go on?

The mother laid her work upon the table, and put her hand up to her face.

"The color hurts my eyes," she said.

The color? Ah, poor Tiny Tim!

"They're better now again," said Cratchit's wife. "Sewing by candlelight makes them weak, and I wouldn't show weak eyes to your father when he comes home, for the world. It must be near his time."

"Past it rather," Peter answered, shutting up his book. "But I think he's walked a little slower than he used, these few last evenings, mother."

They were very quiet again. At last she said, and in a steady cheerful voice, that only faltered once:

"I have known him walk with—I have known him walk with Tiny Tim upon his shoulder, very fast indeed."

"And so have I," cried Peter. "Often."

"And so have I!" exclaimed another. So had all.

"But he was very light to carry," she resumed, intent upon her work, "and his father loved him so, that it was no trouble—no trouble. And there is your father at the door!"

She hurried out to meet him. Bob in his muffler came in. His tea was ready for him on the hob, and they all tried to serve him at once. Then the two young Cratchits got upon his knees and hugged him as if they said, "Don't mind it, Father. Don't be grieved!"

Bob was very cheerful with them, and spoke pleasantly to all the family. He looked at the work upon the table, and praised the hard work and speed of Mrs. Cratchit and the girls. They would be done long before Sunday, he said.

"Sunday! You went today then, Robert?" said his wife.

"Yes, my dear," returned Bob. "I wish you could have gone. It would have done you good to see how green a place it is. But you'll see it often. I promised him that I would walk there on a Sunday. My little, little child!" cried Bob. "My little child!"

He broke down all at once. He couldn't help it. If he could have helped it, he and his child would have been farther apart perhaps than they were.

He left the room, and went up stairs into the room above. It was lighted cheerfully, and decorated for Christmas. There was a chair set close beside the child, and there were signs of some one having been there, lately. Poor Bob sat down in it, and when he had thought a little and composed himself, he kissed the little face. He accepted what had happened, and went down again quite happy.

They drew about the fire, and talked, the girls and mother working still. Bob told them of the extraordinary kindness of Mr. Scrooge's nephew. Bob had only met him once before, but the nephew had recognized him on the street that day. Seeing that he looked a little—"just a little down you know," said Bob, the nephew asked what had happened to upset him. "He is the pleasantest-spoken gentleman you ever heard, so I told him," said Bob. " 'I am heartily sorry for it, Mr. Cratchit,' he said, 'and heartily sorry for your good wife.' By the bye, how he ever knew that, I don't know."

"Knew what, my dear?"

"Why, that you were a good wife," replied Bob.

"Everybody knows that!" said Peter.

"Very well put, my boy!" cried Bob. "I hope they do. 'Heartily sorry,' he said, 'for your good wife. If I can be of service to you in any way,' he said, giving me his card, 'that's where I live. Pray come to me.' Now, it wasn't," cried Bob, "for the sake of anything he might be able to do for us, so much as for his kind way, that this was quite delightful. It really seemed as if he had known our Tiny Tim, and felt sorrow with us."

"I'm sure he's a good soul!" said Mrs. Cratchit.

"You would be surer of it, my dear," returned Bob, "if you saw and spoke to him. I wouldn't be at all surprised, mark what I say, if he got Peter a better job."

"Only hear that, Peter," said Mrs. Cratchit.

"And then," cried one of the girls, "Peter will be keeping company with some one, and setting up for himself."

"Get along with you!" retorted Peter, grinning.

"It's just as likely as not," said Bob, "one of these days. Though there's plenty of time for that, my dear. But however and whenever we part from one another, I am sure we shall none of us forget poor Tiny Tim—shall we—or this first parting that there was among us?"

"Never, Father!" cried they all.

"And I know," said Bob, "I know, my dears, that when we remember how patient and how mild he was, we shall not quarrel easily among ourselves. We would forget poor Tiny Tim in doing it."

"No, never, Father!" they all cried again.

"I am very happy," said Bob, "I am very happy!"

Mrs. Cratchit kissed him, his daughters kissed him, the two young Cratchits kissed him, and Peter and himself shook hands. Spirit of Tiny Tim, your childish essence was from God!

"Spectre," said Scrooge, "something informs me that our parting moment is at hand. I know it, but I know not how. Tell me who was that man whom we saw lying dead?"

The Ghost of Christmas Yet to Come conveyed him, as before—though at a different time, he thought. Indeed, there seemed no order in these visions, except that they were in the Future. They went into the business area, but once again Scrooge did not see himself. Indeed, the Spirit did not stop for anything, but went straight on until Scrooge asked him to wait for a moment.

"This court," said Scrooge, "through which we hurry now, is where my place of occupation is, and has been for a length of time. I see the house. Let me behold what I shall be, in days to come."

The Spirit stopped; the hand was pointed elsewhere.

"The house is yonder," Scrooge exclaimed. "why do you point away?"

The pointing finger did not change.

Scrooge hastened to the window of his office, and looked in. It was an office still, but not his. The furniture was not the same, and the figure in the chair was not himself. The Phantom pointed as before.

Scrooge joined it once again, and wondering where he had gone, accompanied the Spectre until they reached an iron gate. He paused to look round before entering.

A churchyard. Here, then, the wretched man whose name he had now to learn, lay underneath the ground. It was a worthy place. It was walled in by houses and overrun by grass and weeds, the growth of vegetation's death, not life. The place was choked up with too much burying. A worthy place!

The Spirit stood among the graves, and pointed down to one. Scrooge advanced towards it trembling. The Phantom was exactly as it had been, but he dreaded that he saw new meaning in its solemn shape.

"Before I draw nearer to that stone to which you point," said Scrooge, "answer me one question. Are these the shadows of the things that will be, or are they shadows of the things that may be, only?"

Still the Ghost pointed downward to the grave by which it stood.

"Men's courses will foreshadow certain ends, to which, if persevered in, they must lead," said Scrooge. "But if the courses be departed from, the ends will change. Say it is thus with what you show me!"

The Spirit was immovable as ever.

Scrooge crept towards it, trembling as he went. Following the pointing finger of the spirit, he read upon the stone of the neglected grave his own name, EBENEZER SCROOGE.

"Am I that man who lay upon the bed?" he cried, upon his knees.

The finger pointed from the grave to him, and back again.

"No, Spirit! Oh no, no!"

The finger still was there.

"Spirit!" he cried, tight clutching at its robe, "Hear me! I am not the man I was. I will not be the man I must have been if it had been for this experience. Why show me this, if I am past all hope?"

For the first time the hand appeared to shake.

"Good Spirit," he cried, as he fell down on the ground before it, "your nature intercedes for me, and pities me. Assure me that I yet may change these shadows you have shown me, by an altered life!"

The kind hand trembled.

"I will honor Christmas in my heart, and try to keep it all the year. I will live in the Past, the Present, and the Future. The Spirits of all Three shall strive within me. I will not shut out the lessons that they teach. Oh, tell me I may erase the writing on this stone!"

In his agony, he caught the spectral hand. It tried to free itself, but he was strong in his pleading, and held it tight. The Spirit, stronger yet, repulsed him.

Holding up his hands in one last prayer to have his fate reversed, Scrooge saw a change in the Phantom's hood and gown. It shrunk, collapsed, and dwindled down into a bedpost.

STAVE FIVE.

THE END OF IT.

YES! And the bedpost was his own. The bed was his own, the room was his own. Best and happiest of all, the time before him was his own, to make amends in!

"I will live in the Past, the Present, and the Future!" Scrooge repeated, as he scrambled out of bed. "The Spirits of all three shall strive within me. Oh Jacob Marley! Heaven, and the Christmas Time be praised for this! I say it on my knees, old Jacob, on my knees!"

He was so fluttered and so glowing with his good intentions, that his broken voice could hardly be heard. He had been sobbing violently in his conflict with the Spirit, and his face was wet with tears.

"They are not torn down," cried Scrooge, folding one of his bed curtains in his arms, "They are not torn down, rings and all. They are here. I am here. The shadows of the things that would have been may be dispelled. They will be. I know they will!"

His hands were busy with his clothes all this time, turning them inside out, putting them on upside down, tearing them, mislaying them.

"I don't know what to do!" cried Scrooge,

laughing and crying in the same breath. "I am as light as a feather, I am as happy as an angel, I am as merry as a school boy. I am as giddy as a drunken man. A merry Christmas to everybody! A happy New Year to all the world. Hallo here! Whoop! Hallo!"

He had run into the sitting-room and was now standing there, out of breath.

"There's the saucepan that the gruel was in!" cried Scrooge, starting off again, and running round the fireplace. "there's the door, by which the Ghost of Jacob Marley entered! There's the corner where the Ghost of Christmas Present sat! There's the window where I saw the wandering Spirits! It's all right, it's all true, it all happened. Ha ha ha!"

Really, for a man who had been out of practice for so many years, it was a splendid laugh, a most wonderful laugh. The father of a long, long, line of brilliant laughs!

"I don't know what day of the month it is!" said Scrooge. "I don't know how long I've been among the Spirits. I don't know anything. I'm quite a baby. Never mind. I don't care. I'd rather be a baby. Hallo! Whoop! Hallo here!"

He was checked in this transports by the churches ringing out the lustiest peals he had ever heard. Clash, clang, hammer, ding, dong, bell. Bell, dong, ding, hammer, clang, clash! Oh, glorious, glorious!

Running to the window, Scrooge opened it, and put out his head. No fog, no mist, just clear, bright, jovial, stirring, cold. Golden sunlight. Heavenly sky, sweet fresh air, merry bells. Oh, glorious. Glorious!

"What's today?" cried Scrooge, calling downward to a boy in Sunday clothes, who perhaps had
wandered in to look about him.

"EH?" returned the boy, amazed.

"What's today, my fine fellow?" said Scrooge.

"Today!" replied the boy. "Why, CHRISTMAS
DAY."

"It's Christmas Day!" said Scrooge to himself.
"I haven't missed it. The Spirits have done it all in
one night. They can do anything they like. Of
course they can. Of course they can. Hallo, my fine
fellow!"

"Hallo!" returned the boy.

"Do you know the poulterer's, in the next
street but one, at the corner?" Scrooge inquired.

"Of course I do," replied the lad.

"An intelligent boy!" said Scrooge. "A remarkable boy! Do you know whether they've sold the
prize turkey that was hanging up there? Not the
little prize turkey, the big one?"

"What, the one as big as me?" returned the boy.

"What a delightful boy!" said Scrooge. "It's a
pleasure to talk to him. Yes, my lad!"

"It's hanging there now," replied the boy.

"Is it?" said Scrooge. "Go and buy it."

"That's silly!" exclaimed the boy.

"No, no," said Scrooge, "I am in earnest. Go
and buy it, and tell them to bring it here, so that I
may give them the address where they must take
it. Come back with the man, and I'll give you a
shilling. Come back with him in less than five minutes, and I'll give you half-a-crown!"

The boy was off like a shot.

"I'll send it to Bob Cratchit's!" whispered

Scrooge, rubbing his hands, and splitting with a laugh. "He won't know who sent it. It's twice the size of Tiny Tim. No one ever made such a joke as sending it to Bob's will be!"

The hand in which he wrote the address was not a steady one, but write it he did, somehow. He went down stairs to open the street door, ready for the coming of the poulterer's man. As he stood there, waiting for the man's arrival, the knocker caught Scrooge's eye.

"I shall love it as long as I live!" cried Scrooge, patting it with his hand. "I scarcely ever looked at it before. What an honest expression it has in its face! It's a wonderful knocker! Here's the turkey. Hallo! Whoop! How are you! Merry Christmas!"

It was a turkey! He never could have stood upon his legs, that bird. He would have snapped them short off in a minute, like sticks.

"Why, it's impossible to carry that to Camden Town," said Scrooge. "You must have a cab."

The chuckle with which he said this, and the chuckle with which he paid for the turkey, and the chuckle with which he paid for the cab, and the chuckle with which he rewarded the boy, were only to be exceeded by the chuckle with which he sat down breathless in his chair again, and chuckled till he cried.

Shaving was not an easy task, for his hand continued to shake very much. Shaving requires attention, even when you don't dance while you are doing it. But if he had cut the end of his nose off, he would have put a bandage over it and been quite satisfied.

He dressed himself "all in his best," and at last

got out into the streets. The people were by this time pouring forth, as he had seen them with the Ghost of Christmas Present. Walking with his hands behind him, Scrooge regarded every one with a delighted smile. He looked so irresistibly pleasant, in a word, that three or four good-humored fellows said, "Good morning, sir! A merry Christmas to you!" And Scrooge said often afterwards, that of all the happy sounds he had ever heard, those were the happiest in his ears.

He had not gone far, when coming on towards him he beheld the portly gentleman who had walked into his counting house the day before and said, "Scrooge and Marley's, I believe?" It gave him a pang in his heart to think how this old gentleman would look at him when they met. But he knew what he had to do, and he did it.

"My dear sir," said Scrooge, quickening his pace, and taking the old gentleman by both his hands. "How do you do? I hope you succeeded yesterday. It was very kind of you. A merry Christmas to you, sir!"

"Mr. Scrooge?"

"Yes," said Scrooge. "That is my name, and I fear it may not be pleasant to you. Allow me to ask your pardon. And will you have the goodness—" here Scrooge whispered in the gentleman's ear.

"Lord bless me!" cried the gentleman, as if his breath were gone. "My dear Mr. Scrooge, are you serious?"

"If you please," said Scrooge. "Not a farthing less. A great many back payments are included in it, I assure you. Will you do me that favor?"

"My dear sir," said the other, shaking hands

with him. "I don't know what to say to such munifi—"

"Don't say anything, please," retorted Scrooge. "Come and see me. Will you come and see me?"

"I will!" cried the old gentleman. And it was clear he meant to do it.

"Thank you," said Scrooge. "I am much obliged to you. I thank you fifty times. Bless you!"

He went to church, and walked about the streets, and watched the people hurrying to and from, and patted children on the head, and questioned beggars, and looked down into the kitchens of houses, and up to the windows. He found that everything could give him pleasure. He had never dreamed that any walk—that anything—could give him so much happiness. In the afternoon, he turned his steps towards his nephew's house.

He passed the door a dozen times before he had the courage to go up and knock. But he made a dash, and did it.

"Is your master at home, my dear?" said Scrooge to the girl. Nice girl! Very.

"Yes, sir."

"Where is he, my love?" said Scrooge.

"He's in the dining room, sir, along with mistress. I'll show you upstairs, if you please."

"Thank you. He knows me," said Scrooge, with his hand already on the dining room lock. "I'll go in here, my dear."

He turned it gently, and slid his face in, round the door. They were looking at the table (which was spread out in great array). Young housekeepers are always anxious about such things, and like to see that everything is right.

THE END OF IT / 103

"Fred!" said Scrooge.

Dear heart alive, how his niece by marriage started! Scrooge had forgotten, for the moment, about her sitting in the corner with the footstool, or he wouldn't have done it, on any account.

"Why bless my soul!" cried Fred. "Who's that?"

"It's I. Your Uncle Scrooge. I have come to dinner. Will you let me in, Fred?"

Let him in! It is a mercy he didn't shake his arm off. Scrooge felt at home in five minutes. Nothing could be heartier. His niece-in-law looked just the same. So did their friends when they came in. Wonderful party, wonderful games, won-der-ful happiness!

But he was early at the office next morning. Oh, he was early there. If he could only be there first, and catch Bob Cratchit coming late! That was the thing he had set his heart upon.

And he did it? Yes, he did! The clock struck nine. No Bob. A quarter past. No Bob. He was full eighteen minutes and a half late. Scrooge sat with his door wide open, so that he might see him come into the tiny room.

Bob's hat was off before he opened the door, his muffler too. He was on his stool in a jiffy, driving away with his pen, as if he were trying to overtake nine o'clock.

"Hallo!" growled Scrooge, in his accustomed voice as near as he could feign it. "What do you mean by coming here at this time of day?"

"I'm very sorry, sir," said Bob. "I know that I am late."

"You are?" repeated Scrooge. "Yes. I think you are. Step this way, if you please."

"It's only once a year, sir," pleaded Bob, appearing from the other room. "It shall not be repeated. I was making rather merry yesterday, sir."

"Now, I'll tell you what, my friend," said Scrooge, "I am not going to stand this sort of thing any longer. And therefore," he continued, leaping from his stool, and giving Bob such a dig in the waistcoat that he staggered backwards, "and therefore I am about to raise your salary!"

Bob trembled, and got a little nearer to the ruler. He had a momentary idea of knocking Scrooge down with it. He thought he might hold Scrooge down and call to the people in the court-yard for help and a straitjacket.

"A merry Christmas, Bob!" said Scrooge, with an earnestness that could not be mistaken, as he clapped him on the back. "A merrier Christmas, Bob, my good fellow, than I have given you, for many a year! I'll raise your salary, and endeavor to assist your struggling family, and we will discuss your affairs this very afternoon, over a bowl of Christmas punch, Bob! Make up the fires and buy another coal scuttle before you dot another i, Bob Cratchit!"

Scrooge was better than his word. He did it all, and infinitely more. And to Tiny Tim, who did NOT die, he was a second father. He became as good a friend, as good a master, and as good a man, as the good old city knew, or any other good old city, town, or borough, in the good old world. Some people laughed to see the change in him, but he let them laugh, and paid no attention to them. For he was wise enough to know that nothing ever happened on this globe, for good, at which some people did not have their fill of laughter. Knowing that such as these would be blind anyway, he thought it quite as well that they should wrinkle up their eyes in grins. His own heart laughed, and that was quite enough for him.

He had no further meetings with Spirits, but lived up to his promises to them, ever afterwards. It was always said of him, that he knew how to keep Christmas well, if any man alive possessed the knowledge. May that be truly said of us, and all of us! And so, as Tiny Tim observed, God bless us, every one!

REVIEWING YOUR READING

Stave One

FINDING THE MAIN IDEA
1. This part of the book is mostly about
   (A) Scrooge's nephew   (B) Scrooge's business
   (C) the visit of Marley's Ghost   (D) why Scrooge was
   stingy   (E) Scrooge's clerk

REMEMBERING DETAILS
2. Who was Scrooge's partner?
   (A) his nephew   (B) Jacob Marley   (C) his sister
   (D) his lawyer
3. Scrooge's nephew
   (A) asked him for a loan   (B) was rude to him
   (C) was an old friend of Scrooge's clerk   (D) was in a
   bad mood   (E) invited Scrooge to Christmas dinner
4. At the time the story took place, Marley had been dead
   for
   (A) seven years   (B) five years   (C) a week
   (D) a year   (E) two years
5. The door-knocker on Scrooge's front door suddenly
   looked
   (A) rusty   (B) as if it were loose   (C) very old
   (D) like Marley's face   (E) like a lion
6. When Scrooge climbed his stairs, he thought that he saw
   (A) a hearse   (B) a horse   (C) Marley's Ghost
   (D) a lighted fire   (E) a Christmas tree
7. Just before Marley's Ghost appeared,
   (A) Scrooge brushed his teeth   (B) a group of carollers
   came by   (C) the fire went out   (D) bells rang all over
   the house   (E) Scrooge read the newspaper
8. Scrooge asked Marley,
   (A) "Dreadful apparition, why do you trouble me?"
   (B) "Are there no prisons?"   (C) "Why did you get
   married?"   (D) "You'll want all day tomorrow, I
   suppose?"   (E) "You wish to be anonymous?"

9. Marley tells Scrooge that he will be visited by
   (A) his nephew   (B) an old friend   (C) his clerk
   (D) two gentlemen   (E) three spirits

DRAWING CONCLUSIONS

10. Scrooge said "humbug" when people wished him a Merry Christmas because
    (A) he thought that Christmas was nonsensical
    (B) he was stingy   (C) he like to give presents
    (D) he wanted them to sing a Christmas carol
    (E) he did not have any money
11. When Scrooge told Jacob Marley, "There's more of gravy than of grave about you," he meant that
    (A) he had not eaten dinner   (B) he was seeing things because his stomach was upset   (C) he believed that Marley's Ghost was standing in front of him
    (D) he did not like gravy   (E) Marley was too fat
12. The chain that Marley's Ghost wore was
    (A) a reminder of what he had cared most about in life
    (B) made from kind acts he had performed
    (C) a symbol of his business success   (D) a reminder that he was dead   (E) very stylish

IDENTIFYING THE MOOD

13. How did Scrooge's nephew feel about Christmas?
    (A) stingy   (B) angry   (C) bored   (D) happy   (E) upset
14. After the Ghost left, Scrooge felt
    (A) cheerful   (B) afraid   (C) angry   (D) surprised
    (E) eager

USING YOUR REASON

15. Marley's Ghost came to Scrooge in order to
    (A) say "hello"   (B) discuss how the business was doing   (C) persuade Scrooge to change his life
    (D) frighten Scrooge   (E) make all the bells in the house ring

16. If Marley's Ghost had not come to visit, Scrooge would probably have
    (A) rung the bells himself   (B) spent the night listening to Christmas carols   (C) gone to his nephew's house for dinner   (D) spent the night the way he always did   (E) cleaned his room
17. The reason Scrooge had such a small fire in his fireplace was
    (A) the room was too hot already   (B) it was summertime   (C) the coal had not been delivered   (D) coal was very cheap   (E) Scrooge was stingy
18. Scrooge recognized some of the phantoms outside his window because
    (A) he had seen their pictures in the newspaper
    (B) they had been businessmen like himself   (C) they were famous   (D) he had gone to school with them
    (E) they were moaning

THINKING IT OVER
1. Do you think that Scrooge's nephew was a good person? Explain.
2. Charles Dickens had great sympathy for the poor people of his time. How can you tell that this is so?

Stave Two

FINDING THE MAIN IDEA
1. This part of the book is mostly about
    (A) Scrooge's nephew   (B) Marley's Ghost
    (C) the clerk   (D) the visit of the Ghost of Christmas Past   (E) the Ghost of Christmas Present

REMEMBERING DETAILS
2. The Spirit came when the clock struck
    (A) one   (B) two   (C) three   (D) four   (E) twelve

3. What was the strangest thing about The Ghost of Christmas Past?
(A) It seemed to change shape.   (B) It looked like Marley.   (C) It carried a piece of holly in its hand.
(D) It had a stocking for a cap.   (E) It looked like a child.

4. The Ghost took Scrooge to the place where
(A) Scrooge had grown up   (B) Scrooge worked
(C) Scrooge's nephew lived   (D) Scrooge met Marley
(E) Scrooge would die

5. Who came to take the young Scrooge home?
(A) a strange Spirit   (B) the schoolmaster   (C) Marley
(D) a little girl   (E) Mr. Fezziwig

7. Scrooge was apprenticed to
(A) Marley   (B) Mr. Fezziwig   (C) Dick Wilkins
(D) his uncle   (E) the two gentlemen

8. Mr. and Mrs. Fezziwig were
(A) wonderful dancers   (B) mean and nasty
(C) Scrooge's relatives   (D) unwilling to celebrate Christmas   (E) terrible cooks

9. When the Ghost shows Scrooge himself in the prime of his life, Scrooge was
(A) talking to Dick Wilkins   (B) laughing with the Fezziwigs   (C) spending Christmas with his nephew
(D) sitting with a fair young girl   (E) counting his money

10. When Scrooge struggled with the Ghost, he tried to
(A) wrap it up in chains   (B) extinguish its light by pulling the cap over its head   (C) run away
(D) wrestle it to the floor   (E) throw it out the window

DRAWING CONCLUSIONS

11. Why did Scrooge want to see the Ghost of Christmas Past with its cap on?
(A) Scrooge did not want to look at the past.
(B) Scrooge thought the Ghost was ugly.   (C) Scrooge thought it looked too much like Marley.   (D) The weather was very cold, and Scrooge worried about its health.   (E) Scrooge thought that if the Ghost put on its hat, it would leave.

12. As a child, Scrooge liked to read because
(A) he wanted to learn about the world   (B) he could
escape to a fantasy world   (C) he was not good at
dancing   (D) it helped him with his algebra
(E) he did not want to play sports
13. Why was Scrooge's engagement broken?
(A) Scrooge's fiance found another boyfriend.
(B) Scrooge found another girl friend.   (C) Scrooge
loved money more than his fiance.   (D) He could not
afford to get married.   (E) Scrooge did not want to have
a family.

IDENTIFYING THE MOOD
13. How did Scrooge feel about Christmas with the
Fezziwigs?
(A) The happiness created was well worth the cost.
(B) It was a waste of money.   (C) The Fezziwigs were
foolish to dance so much.   (D) Mr. Fezziwig deserved
no praise for his efforts.   (E) Scrooge wanted to do the
same thing when he had employees.
14. As Scrooge saw some of his Christmases of the past, he
felt many feelings. Which is not one of them?
(A) love   (B) sadness   (C) envy   (D) hatred
(E) happiness

USING YOUR REASON
15. When the Ghost said, "My time grows short. Quick," to
whom was it speaking?
(A) Scrooge   (B) the individuals in the Christmas scenes
that were left for Scrooge to see   (C) Little Fan   (D)
Dick Wilkins   (E) Marley's Ghost
16. Why did Scrooge want the Ghost of Christmas Past to
take him away?
(A) Watching the happiness of the young family hurt him
and made him realize what he had lost.   (B) Scrooge was
getting cold.   (C) Scrooge feared his head cold was
worsening.   (D) Scrooge hated to see people happy at
Christmas.   (E) Scrooge wanted a good night's sleep.

18. What was the Ghost of Christmas Past trying to show
    Scrooge?
    (A) It was trying to show Scrooge why Scrooge did not
    like Christmas.   (B) Scrooge did not always dislike
    Christmas.   (C) Christmas could be wonderful.
    (D) Both A and B   (E) A, B, and C

THINKING IT OVER
1. Why did the Ghost of Christmas Past appear both young
   and old?
2. What is ironic in the lovely young woman's statement to
   Scrooge, "You may—the memory of what is past half
   makes me hope you will—have pain in this"?

Stave Three

FINDING THE MAIN IDEA
1. This part of the book is mostly about
   (A) Tiny Tim   (B) Marley's Ghost   (C) the visit of
   the Ghost of Christmas Past   (D) the visit of the Ghost
   of Christmas Present   (E) the visit of the Ghost of
   Christmas Future

REMEMBERING DETAILS
2. The second Spirit came when the clock struck
   (A) one   (B) two   (C) three   (D) four   (E) twelve
3. What was different about the room where Scrooge met
   the second Spirit?
   (A) The room was very cold.   (B) The room was dark.
   (C) The room was filled with green leaves, berries, and
   lots of food.   (D) The room was filled with people.
   (E) The room turned into a frightening graveyard.
4. The second Spirit looked like
   (A) a giant   (B) an angel   (C) a young, but old man
   (D) Santa Claus   (E) an English gentleman
5. The second Spirit wore
   (A) a bright red suit trimmed in white fur   (B) a simple
   deep green robe bordered with fur   (C) a shepherd's
   cloak and staff   (D) a tuxedo with top hat   (E) a coat
   of rags and dirty leather pants

6. Which of the following places did the second Spirit not take Scrooge?
   (A) a church service   (B) a city street   (C) Bob Cratchit's house   (D) the grocer's establishment
   (E) his nephew's Christmas dinner
7. What did Tiny Tim wear on his leg?
   (A) an iron brace   (B) a cast   (C) special support stockings   (D) a knee-length boot   (E) a filthy bandage
8. How did Scrooge's nephew and his family entertain themselves at Christmas?
   (A) They had some music.   (B) They strung cranberries for the tree.   (C) They played children's games.
   (D) two of these   (E) all of these
9. What clung to the folds of the Spirit's robes?
   (A) two hideous children   (B) Tiny Tim   (C) Scrooge   (D) the miner and his family   (E) a bear

DRAWING CONCLUSIONS
10. When the second Spirit said that he had more than eighteen hundred brothers, he meant
    (A) he had a very large family   (B) to impress Scrooge by exaggerating the number of people in his family
    (C) that he had to be very responsible because so many people depended upon him   (D) that there had been more than eighteen hundred Christmases in the past
    (E) all people were brothers
11. Why was the second Spirit pleased that Scrooge wanted to stay at his nephew's feast?
    (A) It showed that Scrooge was beginning to understand the meaning of Christmas.   (B) Scrooge was no longer lazy.   (C) The Spirit was tired because he was growing old, and it appreciated the chance to rest.   (D) The Spirit wanted to humiliate Scrooge by showing him that his family hated him.   (E) The Spirit had no place else to take Scrooge.

12. How do you know that the Cratchits and Scrooge's nephew and his family recognized what kind of person Scrooge was and cared about him anyway?
(A) Scrooge received Christmas cards from both families.   (B) Both families toasted Scrooge at Christmas dinner.   (C) They both invited Scrooge for Christmas dinner.   (D) The Cratchits and the nephew sent Scrooge a Christmas present.   (E) They sang Christmas carols at Scrooge's home.

IDENTIFYING THE MOOD
13. Most of the people in Stave Three are
(A) poor but honest   (B) stingy, like Scrooge
(C) ruddy and pot bellied   (D) anxious and in a hurry
(E) jovial and happy
14. Scrooge's nephew had a wonderful
(A) singing voice   (B) Christmas tree in the parlor
(C) head of hair   (D) present for Scrooge   (E) laugh

USING YOUR REASON
15. How were the scenes at the Cratchits and the nephew's home similar to an earlier scene?
(A) Turkey was the main course for Christmas dinner.
(B) They reminded Scrooge of his school days.
(C) The Spirit forced Scrooge to stay and watch all the family Christmas parties.   (D) They were similar to the happy family Christmas at the Fezziwigs' home.
(E) Each scene made Scrooge say "Bah, humbug!"
16. What did Scrooge mean when he wished that he could have listened to the simple little song sung by his niece-in-law more often?
(A) He enjoyed her lovely voice.   (B) He might have learned the meaning of Christmas earlier.   (C) He could have learned the melody.   (D) His sister could have taught it to him.   (E) He wanted to sing it to Marley.
17. What was the special "ingredient" that the Spirit sprinkled on people's food?
(A) cinnamon   (B) good luck   (C) happiness and joy
(D) protection against evil   (E) long life

114

18. Why did the Spirit grow old so quickly?
(A) Spirits age quickly. (B) The Spirit was exhausted from taking Scrooge so many places. (C) It had used up all its magic potion. (D) It was not really older; it was angry because Scrooge refused to learn its lesson. (E) It lived only one day—Christmas.

THINKING IT OVER
1. What evidence do you have that Scrooge was changing his attitude?
2. Charles Dickens was famous for his social commentary about problems in British society. Toward the end of the stave, what evidence do you find that shows his concern for disadvantaged people?

Stave Four

FINDING THE MAIN IDEA
1. This part of the book is mostly about
(A) Scrooge's nephew (B) the visit of the Ghost of Christmas Past (C) the visit of the Ghost of Christmas Present (D) the visit of the Ghost of Christmas Yet to Come (E) all of the above

REMEMBERING DETAILS
2. Scrooge recognized that the third Spirit had come to
(A) do him good (B) scare him terribly (C) take him to his sister (D) show him how Christmas was celebrated throughout the world (E) force him to help Tiny Tim
3. All Scrooge could see of the third Spirit was its
(A) mouth (B) eyes (C) pointing hand (D) claw-like feet (E) fleshless face
4. The first people this Spirit showed to Scrooge were
(A) a group of businessmen (B) the charwoman, laundress, and the undertaker's man (C) Bob Cratchit's family (D) his nephew and niece-in-law (E) the ghosts of people who had not learned the meaning of Christmas

5. What had the two heavily-burdened women and man dressed in faded black done?
(A) They had stolen from Scrooge. (B) They had refused to attend his funeral. (C) They had borrowed money from Scrooge. (D) They had taken over his business. (E) They buried Scrooge in a lonely grave.

6. The Phantom wanted Scrooge to
(A) remove the cover from the dead man's face
(B) give money to the poor (C) ask the Cratchits for forgiveness (D) sing his sister's song (E) hurry back to his business office

7. What emotion did Caroline and her husband feel when they learned of Scrooge's death?
(A) sadness (B) anger (C) relief (D) disbelief (E) unhappiness

8. Why was the Cratchit household so quiet?
(A) Most of the family had to work on Christmas.
(B) The children had gone to purchase the Christmas goose. (C) They no longer had enough money to celebrate Christmas (D) Tiny Tim had died. (E) The children had serious cases of influenza.

9. As the time for the Ghost to leave approached, the Spirit turned into
(A) a door knob (B) the bed curtains (C) the bedpost (D) the wardrobe (E) the bell pull

DRAWING CONCLUSIONS

10. Why did the businessmen seem unaffected by "Old Scratch's" death?
(A) They did not inherit any money from him.
(B) He had been no one's friend. (C) Dickens was showing his readers that businessmen have no feelings.
(D) Only relatives were to attend the funeral.
(E) The funeral occurred on a business day.

11. Why were Mrs. Dilber and her friends able to sell the dead man's possessions?
    (A) No one cared enough about him to be with him when he died so his things were easily stolen.
    (B) The dead man had given his things to Mrs. Dilber and her friends as a reward.   (C) The items had been discarded by the dead man's relatives because they were almost worthless.   (D) The police had failed to protect the dead man's home.   (E) The people were raising money for the dead man's funeral.
12. Why were Caroline and her husband affected by the man's death?
    (A) They thought that they would inherit all his money.
    (B) The husband worked for Scrooge and feared he would loose his job.   (C) They felt that any new creditor would be kinder and fairer to them than the dead man.   (D) Caroline was happy that she would not have to cook for the man anymore.   (E) They had hoped that the dead man would be the godfather. of their child

IDENTIFYING THE MOOD
13. The third Spirit was
    (A) grave and silent   (B) shrouded in a deep black garment   (C) mysterious and frightening.   (D) two of the above   (C) all of the above
14. How was the third Spirit different from the first two Spirits?
    (A) the third Spirit was female   (B) the third Spirit did not teach Scrooge a lesson   (C) the third Spirit never spoke to Scrooge   (D) there was no truth in what this Spirit showed Scrooge   (E) the third Spirit asked Scrooge to change his ways

USING YOUR REASON

15. How did Scrooge learn the third Spirit's lessons?
    (A) The Spirit told Scrooge the point.   (B) The Spirit
    pointed to words in a special book.   (C) The Phantom
    questioned Scrooge until he came up with the correct
    answers   (D) Scrooge realized them himself as he
    watched what the Spirit showed him   (E) Scrooge did
    not learn any lessons from the third Spirit
16. Why did the Spirit show Scrooge that Tiny Tim had
    died?
    (A) the Spirit wanted Scrooge to feel bad   (B) the
    phantom was a cruel Spirit   (C) Tiny Tim's death was
    inevitable   (D) the Spirit made Scrooge realize that
    more money would help the Cratchits care for the boy
    (E) the Spirit wanted Scrooge to know that family love
    was not important
17. Why did the Spirit not assure Scrooge that he could
    change what he had seen happening in the futureif he
    changed his ways?
    (A) It was important for Scrooge to change because he
    wanted to become a better person.   (B) The Spirit had
    no voice.   (C) The future could not be changed.
    (D) Scrooge refused to admit that he had been wrong.
    (E) The Spirit knew that Scrooge would soon be dead.
18. What does the Spirit of Christmas symbolize for
    Scrooge?
    (A) a time to spend too much money   (B) a time to eat
    a great deal of food and to be with family
    (C) a ridiculous holiday   (D) a time to take advantage
    of other people's kindness   (E) kindness and love for
    other people

THINKING IT OVER

1. Why did it take so long for Scrooge to recognize that he
   was the dead man people were talking about?
2. Why was the Ghost of Christmas Future so different
   from the other two Christmas Spirits?

Stave Five

FINDING THE MAIN IDEA

1. This part of the book is mostly about
   (A) Scrooge's nephew   (B) Scrooge's change in
   behavior   (C) the Cratchits   (D) the visit of the
   Ghost of Christmas Past   (E) the Ghost of Christmas
   Future

REMEMBERING DETAILS

2. Scrooge awakens on what day?
   (A) Christmas Eve   (B) Christmas Day
   (C) the day after Christmas   (D) New Year's Eve
   (E) New Year's Day
3. What does Scrooge buy to send to the Cratchits?
   (A) a Christmas feast   (B) a roasted goose
   (C) an enormous turkey   (D) a delicious Christmas
   pudding   (E) a wonderful Christmas tree
4. Whom does Scrooge visit the day after the third Spirit's
   stay?
   (A) The Cratchits   (B) Mrs. Dilber   (C) Caroline and
   her husband   (D) the Marley family   (E) his nephew
5. What did Scrooge do to Bob Cratchit the day after
   Christmas?
   (A) Scrooge fired him.   (B) Scrooge promised Tiny
   Tim a college education.   (C) Scrooge gave him a
   raise.   (D) Scrooge made him work overtime to make
   up for Christmas off.   (E) Scrooge promoted him.

DRAWING CONCLUSIONS

6. Why did Scrooge praise Jacob Marley?
   (A) Scrooge missed his old partner.   (B) Scrooge was
   happy that Marley had sent him the Spirits.
   (C) Scrooge realized that he had not said any prayers for
   his partner.   (D) Scrooge was afraid of Marley's Ghost.
   (E) Scrooge had become very religious after his
   experience with the Ghosts.

7. What did Scrooge realize when he noticed that his bed curtains were not torn down?
(A) He realized that he could change the future by changing his behavior. (B) He knew that he was not dead. (C) He saw that the curtains had not been stolen. (D) He knew that his cold would get better. (E) He was happy that he would not have to buy another set of curtains .

8. What did Scrooge promise the portly man?
(A) Scrooge promised to go to church on Sundays.
(B) Scrooge let him collect the money on Caroline's loan. (C) Scrooge promised to sell him a very large turkey. (D) Scrooge gave the man a large charitable contribution. (E) Scrooge promised the man a partnership in his business.

9. From Scrooge's actions, what do you assume about his future?
(A) The future predicted by the Ghost of Christmas Yet to Come would come true. (B) Scrooge would return to his old ways. (C) Scrooge would not end up the way the Ghost of Christmas Future had shown.
(D) Scrooge would die soon. (E) He would fire Bob Cratchit.

IDENTIFYING THE MOOD

10. What is Scrooge's mood when he awakened the morning after the Ghost of Christmas Future's visit?
(A) joyful and merry (B) furious and mean (C) tired and confused (D) sad and upset (E) ill and depressed

11. What does Scrooge's teasing Cratchit show?
(A) a new child-like side of Scrooge's personality
(B) that he had become insane (C) Scrooge's mean streak (D) Bob Cratchit was in trouble. (E) Scrooge hated Bob Cratchit.

USING YOUR REASON

12. What does Scrooge's wonderful laugh indicate?
    (A) He had already changed into a better person.
    (B) He was crazy. (C) His fever was so high that he
    was delirious. (D) He was close to death.
    (E) He was afraid of the Ghosts.

13. Which of the following was <u>not</u> an action that showed
    Scrooge had changed?
    (A) his tip to the boy   (B) his dressing in his best
    clothes   (C) his visit to church   (D) his trip to the
    cemetery   (E) his cheerfulness with his nephew

14. Why was Scrooge's niece-in-law startled at Christmas
    dinner?
    (A) She was afraid of Scrooge.   (B) She did not expect
    him to come to dinner.   (C) Scrooge looked very ill.
    (D) Scrooge's singing voice was terrible.
    (E) She hated being surprised.

THINKING IT OVER

1. What is the theme or message of The Christmas Carol?